The Medieval Worlds of Neil Gaiman

THE Medieval Worlds OF Neil Gaiman

From *Beowulf* to Sleeping Beauty

SHILOH CARROLL

University of Iowa Press • Iowa City

University of Iowa Press, Iowa City 52242

uipress.uiowa.edu
Printed in the United States of America

Cover design by Kimberly Glyder
Text design and typesetting by April Leidig

Printed on acid-free paper

Library of Congress Cataloging-in-Publication Data
Names: Carroll, Shiloh, 1980– author.
Title: The Medieval Worlds of Neil Gaiman: From Beowulf to Sleeping Beauty / by Shiloh Carroll.
Description: Iowa City: University of Iowa Press, [2023] | Includes bibliographical references and index.
Identifiers: LCCN 2022059912 (print) | LCCN 2022059913 (ebook) | ISBN 9781609389130 (paperback; acid-free paper) | ISBN 9781609389147 (ebook)
Subjects: LCSH: Gaiman, Neil—Criticism and interpretation. | Medievalism in literature. | Literature, Medieval—Influence. | LCGFT: Literary criticism.
Classification: LCC PR6057.A319 Z594 2023 (print) | LCC PR6057.A319 (ebook) | DDC 823/.914—dc23/eng/20230113
LC record available at https://lccn.loc.gov/2022059912
LC ebook record available at https://lccn.loc.gov/2022059913

CONTENTS

The Medieval Worlds of Neil Gaiman

INTRODUCTION

Neil Gaiman and Medievalism

A 630-year-old man walks into a Renaissance fair and proceeds to complain that it's not realistic enough. "It's someone's idea of the English Middle Ages crossed with bloody Disneyland," he declares.[1] He fusses to anyone who will listen that there's not enough shit or pox, the beer is too weak, and the minstrels are annoying.

Hob Gadling isn't just a cranky old man; he's a cranky old man who has lived through the Middle Ages, the Enlightenment, the early modern period, all the way up to the twentieth century. His creator, Neil Gaiman, uses him in *Sandman* to demonstrate how cultural memory storifies the past, particularly the Middle Ages. Gaiman uses Hob to briefly describe medievalism, but there's more to medievalism than misunderstanding the Middle Ages, just as there's more to Neil Gaiman than *Sandman*.

Chances are if you're into genre fiction at all—and, let's be honest, even if you're not—you've heard of Gaiman. In his forty-year career, he has written work that spans media (TV, movies, radio, novels, short stories, graphic novels), genres (science fiction, fantasy, horror, nonfiction, superheroes), and age ranges (picture books, middle grade, young adult, and adult). His print work has been adapted to television, film, radio, and stage; some has even crossed media, with prose or poetic works being adapted into graphic novels or illustrated editions. He has been awarded three honorary doctorates, five Hugos, two Nebulas, four Bram Stoker awards, twenty-two Locus awards, and Newbery and Carnegie medals, among dozens of others. Yet he still finds time to interact with 2.9 million Twitter followers, a constant stream of questions on Tumblr, and Q&As at book tours. As the *New York Times*' Sarah Lyall puts it, Gaiman "exists in the centre of a rare Venn diagram where bestselling author meets famous personality meets cult figure."[2]

Neil Richard Gaiman was born in England in 1960 to a Polish Jewish family who also practiced Scientology. He has said, however, that he is not a practicing Scientologist, and that Judaism is "the religion of his family."[3] He learned to read at age four and has listed his favorite authors as J. R. R. Tolkien, C. S. Lewis, and Lewis Carroll. In an interview with his daughter, Maddy, he said that his first piece of writing was a poem composed at age three, transcribed by his mother.[4] As he grew up, his favorite authors expanded to include Mary Shelley, Rudyard Kipling, Ursula K. Le Guin, and G. K. Chesterton, although Roger Zelazny has had the most direct impact both on his style and career.[5]

His writing career began in journalism, not fiction. His first book was a biography of the band Duran Duran, published in 1984, which he has since said he wishes he'd never written because he wrote it for money that never materialized and it wasn't even something he'd have read.[6] He continued to work as a journalist for several years, publishing another nonfiction book, in 1986, before becoming disillusioned with British journalism and moving more permanently to fiction.

Gaiman's first major fiction publications were in comic books. He wrote for several DC Comics series before being hired to resurrect an old character: the Sandman. Instead of the pulp detective version that had previously appeared in *Sandman* titles, Gaiman created Morpheus, the anthropomorphic representation of dreams—a character far from the usual butt-kicking DC Comics superhero. Gaiman did not expect the series to last long, noting that every comic he had liked working on had been a "commercial failure."[7] So he took on big ideas, writing treatments for comic scripts he never thought he'd be allowed to draft.[8]

Then *Sandman* began selling.

It outsold *Swamp Thing* and Hellblazer, DC Comics' most popular adult titles. Then it outsold *Batman* and *Superman*. Between 1991 and 1999, *Sandman* won twenty Eisner Awards, four of those for writing.[9] In 2000, it was nominated for a Hugo for best related work.[10] The success put incredible pressure on Gaiman, who noted, "*Sandman* has gradually gotten to the point of being what I'm automatically linked to and thought of by people as the creator of. [. . .] And I know that, for my sanity, the story is going to have to end. But that doesn't make it easier."[11] Two years later, in a 1996 interview, Gaiman worried about his fame and cult appeal, saying he intended to "spend a couple of years doing other things [. . .] and go back to comics when people have forgotten me."[12] *Sandman*'s initial run ended in March 1996 with seventy-five total issues, and editor Karen Berger made the unprecedented decision to end the series rather than bring on another writer to continue it.[13] Yet as history has shown, Gaiman was anything but forgotten after leaving *Sandman*.

While writing *Sandman*, Gaiman was also collaborating with Terry Pratchett on *Good Omens*, a humorous take on the apocalypse, which was published in 1990. He followed this with his novelization of the TV serial *Neverwhere* (1996), which he had also written, while continuing to write and edit comics. Soon after came the novels *Stardust* (1999) and *American Gods* (2001).

Gaiman was now well and truly established. Since then, hardly a year has gone by that hasn't seen some release of his work somewhere, whether in comics, prose, television, film, or radio. He writes original fiction and contributes to established worlds like Doctor Who. He adapts his own work into different formats (*Good Omens* to television) or allows others to do the same (*The Ocean at the End of the Lane* to stage). And occasionally he goes back to *Sandman* and writes another new story for it.

The wide variation in Gaiman's work can be explained by his approach to inspiration. Gaiman encourages writers to create a "compost heap"—somewhere to put small incidents, ideas, people, bits of conversation, and other influences—that will blend into a stew that can be used to create stories.[14] This is similar to J. R. R. Tolkien's idea of the soup pot, a simmering vat of stew that collects stories for writers to draw from. Though Tolkien's pot is more universal and historical than Gaiman's more personal compost heap, the idea is basically the same: inspiration comes from everywhere and everything. Gaiman gathers everything he can as he goes through life and uses it to tell stories.

Modern fantasy, possibly more than any other genre, is a compost heap of heavy medieval influences. Gaiman follows a robust and deep tradition of a magical Middle Ages, influenced by people such as J. R. R. Tolkien, William Morris, and Sir Walter Scott. Their influences can be traced back further, through the Brothers Grimm and Sir Thomas Malory, and even into medieval epics such as *Beowulf*—which itself can be traced even further into Greek and Roman mythology, and so on, back into prehistory. Literature endlessly builds on itself.

For the sake of clarity, let me explain a few terms that I'll be using extensively, beginning with the difference between medieval and medievalism. "Medieval" or "the Middle Ages" refers to the historical time period between about 500 and 1500 CE, along with the era's attendant cultural expressions, like literature, politics, and religion. In contrast, medievalism is a postmedieval (after 1500 CE) interpretation of the medieval. Any meaning assigned to medieval culture or texts after the Middle Ages is by definition a medievalist one. People who study the history of the Middle Ages are called medievalists, while something derived from the Middle Ages can be called medievalist; the people who study medievalism are sometimes called medievalismists. One of the earliest examples of such interpretation is Francesco Petrarch's (1304–74)[15] declaring this period the Dark Ages, understood as a time of ignorance and barbarism that descended on the world after the fall of Rome.[16] Dating historical periods can be fuzzy; for Petrarch, the early fourteenth century was the beginning of the Italian Renaissance. Yet the Middle Ages are considered to continue for another 200 years because the English Renaissance, for example, is dated to the late fifteenth century. Dating the Middle Ages as 500 CE (the end of the western Roman Empire) to 1500 CE (around the time Columbus sailed for the Americas) is fairly arbitrary. Petrarch's declaration tells us more about his own prejudices than it does about the Middle Ages, but projecting assumptions backward is a core facet of medievalism.

Academics will also often distinguish between medievalism and neomedievalism. The latter, much slipperier, term is usually used for even less medieval medievalism, like fantasy novels that get their version of the Middle Ages from Tolkien, or purposefully inaccurate or playful portrayals of the Middle Ages, such as the 2001 film *A Knight's Tale* or the ABC TV series *Galavant* (2015–16). Just to keep things from getting too muddy, I use "medievalism" for any postmedieval-period interpretation of the medieval period or medieval culture.

None of these terms is meant judgmentally; neomedievalism isn't "worse" medievalism. The terms exist to help explain how many levels of separation sit between a text (or cultural phenomenon, or idea) and the historical Middle Ages. For the purposes of this book, I care very little about accuracy in Gaiman's portrayal of the Middle Ages—mostly because Gaiman isn't usually attempting any, but also because a fully accurate portrayal of the Middle Ages in fantasy is impossible. Fantasy is transformative; it's meant to ask "what if" questions and introduce magic into an unmagical system. Also, there are so many layers of history, literature, art, and architecture, among other artifacts, between now and the Middle Ages that it's nearly impossible to put ourselves into the mind-set of a person from the Middle Ages. And this isn't even getting into the problem of referring to a thousand-year, multicountry, multicontinent span of time as though it were a single unified era and culture.[17]

Western fantasy literature is deeply medievalist. Early influences in the genre came from courtly romances, especially Arthurian romances, and Celtic fairy stories. Early modern writers such as Edward Spenser (*The Faerie Queen*, 1590), Charles Perrault (*Histories, or Tales of Past Times*, 1697), and even Shakespeare (*A Midsummer Night's Dream*, 1594) pulled on these medieval stories for their works. In the Gothic tradition, which began around 1760, medievalism was more overtly political. Writers such as Horace Walpole (*The Castle of Otranto*, 1764) projected their distrust in Enlightenment ideas backward into a vague idea of the Middle Ages—the dark, gritty version—in order to avoid falling prey to sedition acts. The pendulum swung the other way for the Romantics, who saw a much more beautiful and sublime Middle Ages. Writers and artists such as John Keats, Samuel Taylor Coleridge, and William Blake influenced the genre with epic language, exoticism, and bright colors.

All these laid the foundation for arguably the most influential medievalismists of the Victorian era: the Pre-Raphaelite Brotherhood, a group of artists, writers, poets, amateur historians, and models whose aesthetic was purposefully medieval. They saw themselves as a second Round Table, "a model of chivalry, courage, loyalty, and mutual support."[18] The Brotherhood produced works such as Christina and Dante Gabriel Rossetti's *Goblin Market* (1862), John Everett Millais's painting *Ophelia* (1852), and the many and varied works of William Morris. Pre-Raphaelites and artists connected to the Pre-Raphaelites have been listed as influences on Lord Dunsany (*The King of Elfland's Daughter*, 1924), J. R. R. Tolkien, and C. S. Lewis.[19]

Because of these medievalisms, various ideas and beliefs about the Middle Ages—as well as style, themes, motifs, and symbols attributed, however correctly or incorrectly, to the period—have been baked into fantasy literature. Even urban fantasy borrows medievalisms; fairies, occultism, and vampires dominate the genre. This is the environment Gaiman is writing in: a multilayered, pseudo-historical, sometimes contradictory semimedieval fantasy tradition. Although Gaiman's approach doesn't quite reach outright medieval high fantasy, by which I mean the kind of medieval we see in, say, George R. R. Martin's *A Song of Ice and Fire*, it is no less medievalist for all that. Gaiman's influences are many, varied, and layered, but as I'll show in the following chapters, medieval and medievalist traditions heavily influence nearly all his work. Yet his work is also distinctly modern. He expertly blends medievalist tropes and themes with current ones, creating stories that consciously borrow from and build on all the stories that have influenced him over the years. Recognizing these influences, both direct and abstract, can deepen and enrich a reader's appreciation of his work. Let's dig deep into Gaiman's compost heap and explore the foundational medieval and medievalist influences on some of his most popular works. These ancient texts still impact our literature today.

CHAPTER ONE

Sandman and Everyman

Morpheus, Lord of Dream, Prince of Stories, son of Time and Night, billions of years old and unbelievably powerful, is *sulking*. Having been freed from a seventy-year imprisonment at the hands of a sorcerer, and then the sorcerer's son, he has faced down rogue dreams, Hell itself, and an escapee from Arkham Asylum to regain the trappings of his power. Now, quest over, he sits in a city square, feeding the birds—and sulking.

This is where his sister, Death, finds him. She gives him a good scolding: "You are *literally* the stupidest, most *self-centered*, appallingest *excuse* for an *anthropomorphic personification* on *this* or any *other* plane!"[1] While Morpheus's nature as Lord of Dream has been indicated in earlier issues,[2] this is the first time in *Sandman* that the phrase "anthropomorphic personification" is used to describe Morpheus and his siblings. It won't be the last. Much of the series is an exploration of what it means to be an allegory and the personification of an idea, as well as what the rules and responsibilities for them are. Intertwined with the lives of the Endless are the lives, struggles, and lessons of mortals, all contributing to the life and ultimately death of Morpheus, Lord of Dreams.

Interaction between humans and personified virtues, vices, and ideas has a long, rich literary and dramatic history. In late medieval/early Tudor England, a specific genre of drama sprang up in response to a variety of religious and social pressures: the morality play. Several of them are still available to us today. The one most frequently anthologized for high school and college literature texts is *The Summoning of*

Everyman, but just as important and useful for this discussion are *The Castle of Perseverance* and *Mankind*. Morality plays had several unifying features: a core (Christian) moral lesson, allegorical personifications of human traits and external pressures, and instructions for living well so that one could also die well. These plays forced an avatar of humankind—Everyman, Humanum Genus, and Mankind, respectively—to face their own faults, sins, and virtues as a warning to the audience. Death can come at any time, they warn; have you lived your life so that you're ready?

Gaiman does not overtly embrace a single religious worldview in *Sandman*, but the series has notable similarities in structure, theme, and motifs to medieval morality plays. The most obvious is the Endless themselves, anthropomorphic personifications of human impulses and psyche. But *Sandman* also contains a core moral lesson intertwined with various approaches to facing death. Death is the inevitable, ultimate end for everything and everyone, even the Endless. Gaiman describes the basic plot of *Sandman* as "the Lord of Dreams learns that one must change or die, and makes his decision."[3] Morality plays explored the effects of one's actions in life on the outcome of one's death, and in its way, *Sandman* does the same, but with enough modern storytelling to keep Morpheus from being simply a flat allegory. He is both allegory *and* compelling character, a skillful use of medieval tropes updated for a modern audience's expectations.

....

MORAL LESSONS

Morality plays were tools for teaching a largely illiterate populace about the various pitfalls that could prevent them from reaching Heaven after death. Religious and political pressure heavily influenced the vices illustrated on stage—after all, this was a time of serious social upheaval. The Protestant Reformation was on the horizon and feudalism was collapsing. As medievalist John Watkins explains, morality playwriters "adopted allegory as their basic mode because its subordination of the particular to the universal mirrored the hierarchies of an imagined feudal polity that equated social aspiration with pride"; the playwrights discouraged the idea of social mobility and insisted on a "predetermined social structure."[4] Not only did morality plays reinforce certain religious concepts, they also used allegories for feudal structures as a foundation to illustrate humankind's relationship with God—and in turn to hint at a divine endorsement for the feudal system itself.[5]

For example, the primary antagonists in the medieval morality play *Mankind* are Mischief, Nought, Nowadays, and New Guise (Fashion); using these personifications, the play warns against novelty and idleness.[6] Ultimately, the "distraction vices" are replaced by a literal devil, serving to show that a fascination with the things of the world leads to damnation. *The Castle of Perseverance* focuses more broadly on the Seven Deadly Sins, casting the struggle for Humanum Genus as a siege in which the everyman is mostly a spectator—not being a knight or lord—rather than an active participant in the battle. And *Everyman* relies heavily on the language of accounting; Everyman must balance his ledger before he dies to show that he has been responsible with his life and earned his place in heaven.

Much of the political and social overtones of these morality plays has been lost to time, as so much of the medieval mind-set has been. While modern readers might see *Everyman* as an overly simplistic, heavy-handed allegory, medievalist V. A. Kolve has teased out layers of meaning that would have been evident to its original audience—that is to say, anyone familiar with the Parable of the Talents from Matthew 25 and its commentaries from writers like St. Jerome.[7] Matthew 25:14–30 recounts Jesus telling his followers that the Kingdom of God is like a man who goes on a journey, leaving his servants with various amounts of money. When he returns, two of them have doubled their money and are praised as good and faithful servants. The third hides his in the ground and is scolded because he could at least have put it in the bank and gotten interest back; the implication is that the servant is sent to Hell. Without these stories and analyses in the common zeitgeist, we lose the experience and understanding of these plays that the medieval viewer would have had. However, even if most of the original context and intertextuality—that is, the interplay of the text in question and its predecessors, and how that interplay helps to shape the meaning of the text—of these plays is no longer accessible (except to those who study medieval writings), their core moral lessons are still visible. Similarly, *Sandman* is heavily intertextual—so much so that between 2012 and 2015, DC Comics released a four-volume set of *The Annotated Sandman,* in which Leslie Klinger meticulously documented thousands of references to other works, historical events, philosophies, and others. Despite this plethora of antecedents and sources, a core moral is evident in the series.

In *Mankind,* the playwright warns us that constant vigilance is necessary to hold off evil. This lesson is achieved through rampant chaos and distraction onstage, as well as purposeful nonsense words and phrases meant to undermine Mercy's preaching and advice. Nought, Nowadays, and New Guise tease Mercy for being a stick-in-the-mud, with his flowery language and knowledge of Latin. "Hey, you, translate *this* into Latin," Nowadays says (roughly glossed): "I have eaten a dishful of curds / And I have shit [or shut] your mouth full of turds."[8] The Worldlings, as the three are called, also use Latin, the language of the church, to say things like "Kiss my ass!" and echo the language of confession and penance for further rude instructions—"Pope Pokett guarantees that if you put your nose in his wife's socket [vagina], you will have forty days of pardon."[9] The staging is purposeful; it distracts, and thus condemns the audience as well. It takes only a moment of distraction for Mankind to fall prey to the demon Titivillus; he then requires reeducating by Mercy before the play's end.[10]

A similar theme emerges in the early issues of *Sandman.* In the first major arc, *Preludes and Nocturnes* (issues 1–8), Morpheus is captured by human mages and imprisoned for seventy-two years. During this time, several of his more terrible nightmares—the Corinthian, Brute, and Glob—get loose and begin terrorizing humans. A good bit of the second major arc, *The Doll's House* (issues 9–16), follows Morpheus as he rounds up and defeats his creations. Several plot and character elements of these issues of *Sandman* show interesting parallels with *Mankind*.

Morpheus's imprisonment was possible in the first place because he was exhausted after fixing a rift in the space-time continuum, much like Mankind's distraction comes when Titivillus steals his spade while he's working. The escaped nightmares Glob and Brute are trying to build their own version of Morpheus's realm, the Dreamtime, in the mind of a traumatized boy, in hopes of creating and ruling a new Dreamtime through a surrogate. Like *Mankind*'s Worldlings, Brute and Glob are given less sophisticated speech mannerisms: "Festering scabs!" Glob complains when Morpheus finds them. "Pus and pox and puke on it all! We came so damned close. Just a few more years. It would have worked."[11] The Corinthian is much more articulate and a bigger threat than Brute and Glob; rather than confining his influence to a single boy, he has been influencing and inspiring serial killers across America. He tells them that they are special, warriors and artists, above the rest of humankind. When Morpheus removes him, they lose their confidence and slink back into the darkness. Hunting the escaped nightmares is simultaneously a distraction from and inextricably linked to Morpheus's quest to find the dream vortex, which could destroy the boundaries between the Dreamtime and the real world.

THE ENDLESS AS ALLEGORICAL PERSONIFICATION

Probably the most famous contemporary example of allegorical fiction is the Chronicles of Narnia (1950–56), C. S. Lewis's portal fantasy series that places Christian theology in a world of high magic, complete with creation story, sacrificial god, and Armageddon. Of course, allegorical personification is an ancient storytelling and rhetorical device, one far predating Lewis. Modern authors use it differently than medieval authors and playwrights; medievalist Pamela King points out that while allegories such as John Bunyan's *Pilgrim's Progress* (1678) and George Orwell's *Animal Farm* (1945) have literal story lines that are separable from their message, in medieval morality plays, the story lines are "the actualisation on stage of their moral 'sentence,'" or lesson.[12] In other words, while we can read modern allegories just for the story while ignoring the deeper lesson, in morality plays, the story is literally the lesson, so no separation is possible.

The central conceit of these plays is giving ideas, qualities, and human attributes a body and letting them speak for themselves. In *Everyman*, characters such as Death, Fellowship, and Good Deeds discuss the fate of Everyman, who is attempting to find someone to accompany him on a pilgrimage (death) from which he will never return. In *Mankind*, New Guise, Nought, and Nowadays attempt to turn Mankind to sin and suicide against the advice of Mercy. And in *The Castle of Perseverance*, Humanum Genus is placed in a castle and defended from the Seven Deadly Sins by the Seven Moral Virtues. In short, the drama of morality plays was "personified virtues and vices contend[ing] over passive protagonists incapable of understanding or ameliorating their circumstances."[13]

While to modern audiences these plays read as unsophisticated and naive, their use of allegory was seen to serve an important purpose. As cognition and literature scholar Jean Bocharova puts it, personification in the Middle Ages "embodied ideas [. . .] and, in the most basic sense, were seen as either making those ideas more palatable, more easily comprehended, or as veiling them in obscurity, both as protection against profane minds and as a reward for the worthy."[14] In other words, allegorical personification helped to clarify some fairly complicated religious ideas—but only for those who were ready and willing to understand them. Comprehending the allegory was its own reward.

Allegorical personification is not unique to medieval morality plays but actually a fundamental way the human brain understands concepts—for example, Justice as a blindfolded woman with a sword and scales.[15] In *Sandman*, Gaiman creates a family of anthropomorphized ideas who are fully aware of their status as such. They are called the Endless: Dream, Destiny, Death, Desire, Delirium, Despair, and Destruction. The Endless rule over their respective realms and interact with humans—and sometimes nonhumans, such as fairies, cats, gods, and stars. Like the personifications in morality plays, they represent fundamental and constant aspects of the human psyche and life cycle; Gaiman describes them as "an attempt to create gods (though they are not gods), anthropomorphic personifications, what-have-you, that would feel relevant today; an unlikely metaphor that could be used as a way of seeing the world."[16]

To illustrate how universal the Endless are, Gaiman links his Lord of Dream to the Greek god Oneiros, the Roman god Morpheus, and the European folk figure of the Sandman. Dream is all of them. Like any allegorical personification, the Endless are fundamentally themselves; they are incapable of change without severe consequences. Morpheus's changing and then rectifying his mistakes ultimately leads to his death. Other Endless have made different decisions: Destruction abandons his realm and duties entirely; Delight, under circumstances not made clear, becomes Delirium; and the current incarnation of Despair was once something else but took on the mantle when the old Despair died.

For the most part, Gaiman allows the names of the Endless to explain their natures, but on two occasions, he pauses for a more thorough overview. The first is in the *Season of Mists* prologue, in which each Endless is formally introduced with a poetic overview—except Death, who, one assumes, needs no introduction.[17] But even these descriptions can't do the concepts behind these personifications justice, he acknowledges: "We perceive but aspects of the Endless, as we see the light glinting from one tiny facet of some huge and flawlessly cut precious stone."[18] The second is in a later collection, *Endless Nights*, in which each Endless gets a short treatment demonstrating a core personality. Characters periodically pause to try to explain what the Endless are, although often their explanations tell us more about the character in question than the Endless. For example, Destruction, who is more frequently referred to as brother or the Prodigal because he has abandoned his post, justifies his refusal to act as Destruction by arguing, "The Endless are merely patterns. The Endless are wave functions. The Endless are repeating motifs."[19] In other words, the Endless are not people but are instead ideas, forces of nature, and figures from the collective unconscious. Destruction's argument is that the Endless are meaningless, and therefore his abdication of his role is also meaningless and hurts nothing in the long run.

If that were true, however, we wouldn't have a story. In *Sandman*, as in most allegory, the Endless are fundamental to human existence, and humanity is fundamental to theirs. The personifications and humanity are in a symbiotic feedback loop. We see this too in *Everyman*, for example, when Everyman petitions Good Deeds to go with him on his journey. "Here I lie, cold in the ground," Good Deeds tells him. "Your sins have me so weighed down that I can't move."[20] Good Deeds's ability to protect Everyman depends on his actions, which up to now haven't given her much sustenance. Rather, he has strengthened Goods (wealth), Fellowship, and Kindred, none of whom can go with him; Goods will, in fact, actively hinder him on his journey. In order to remedy this, Everyman performs acts of contrition and penance, removing the weight of sin that weakens Good Deeds and prevents her from traveling into the afterlife with him.

Sandman is full of the same interconnectedness between humans and the supernatural. Gaiman follows a traditional idea usually paraphrased as "as above, so below," which basically means that different planes of existence can have direct effects on each other.[21] Morpheus's actions or situation can influence the world, and humans can influence the Dreamtime, just as the actions of humans in morality plays are shown to affect the personifications of metaphysical ideas, which in turn affects the humans' afterlife.

Gaiman establishes Morpheus's importance to not only the Dreaming but also to the world at large early in the story, when Morpheus is trapped by a ritual meant to capture Death. In the seventy years of Morpheus's imprisonment, a not insubstantial number of people fall asleep and don't wake up. Others can't sleep at all. Several lose their dreams and feel bereft, as though "something died inside [them] a long time ago."[22] With Morpheus separated from his realm, unable to perform his duties, the sleeping and dreaming patterns of people all over the world are thrown into disarray. A similar state of chaos descends after Morpheus's release, when John Dee acquires Morpheus's ruby, one of the tools of his power. Dee uses it to "dredge up the blackness from their souls," creating a world of waking nightmares and driving everyone mad.[23] Morpheus's very existence is what keeps humans' sleeping and dreaming in order; without him, the world suffers.

We also see humans influence the Dreamtime. In *The Doll's House,* Rose Walker arises as what Gaiman calls a dream vortex, the very existence of which can collapse the boundaries of Dream, perhaps even destroy it. But even nonsupernaturally endowed people influence Dream. While part of Morpheus's job is creating creatures and landscapes for humans to dream in, frequently people's own imaginations can create these landscapes without his input. This idea is most prominent in *A Game of You,* the fourth major story arc in *Sandman,* in which recurring character Barbie lucid-dreams her way through the Land to rescue it and her dream friends from the Cuckoo. "There must be *hundreds* of these lands," the Cuckoo explains. "An archipelago of dream-islands, a glittering shoal of worlds. [. . .] Little Barbie found the land she needed . . . and The Land found someone to believe in it."[24] While Morpheus refers to himself as the creator of the Land, he also acknowledges to Lucien that he had forgotten it even existed.[25] Without his input or interference, it continued to exist with the help of humans like Barbie.

In "Lost Hearts," the last chapter of *The Doll's House*, Gaiman has Rose Walker and Morpheus voice opposing views of the human–Endless relationship. Rose sees it as ultimately abusive:

> We're just dolls. We don't have a clue, what's really going down, we just kid ourselves that we're in control of our lives while a paper's thickness away things that would drive us mad if we thought about them for too long play with us, and move us around from room to room, and put us away at night when they're tired, or bored.[26]

Rose, having been through an incredibly traumatic experience that revealed the Endless to her, is understandably upset about the existence of gods, magic, and the Endless and what that means for her worldview, especially when it comes to free will. Morpheus, however, sees the relationship between humankind and the Endless quite differently: "We of the Endless are servants of the living—we are *not* their masters. We exist because they know, deep down, in their hearts, that we exist."[27] Like the morality play personifications, they are aspects of the human psyche given body and voice. The Endless do not control us; they *are* us, collectively and individually. The metaphysical structure of the *Sandman* universe echoes philosophy and religion from ancient and medieval thinkers that was distilled into the exhortations of the medieval morality play.

LIVING WELL TO DIE WELL

Because nothing in Gaiman's work is ever just one thing, it's possible to read Morpheus as an everyman figure—not in the sense that he is meant to represent all of humankind, as Everyman, Mankind, and Humanum Genus are, but in the sense that he is the central figure in a story filled with allegory and morality. Every part of *Sandman* shows us how Morpheus has failed to be kind, humble, or forgiving, then follows his attempts to atone for his mistakes before he dies, even as those mistakes are the reason for his death. Like *Everyman*, the story begins not far from the chronological end of Morpheus's life, but it provides memories, flashbacks, and encounters with figures from his past that establish how he has conducted himself over his billions of years—and it's not always good.

After establishing Morpheus as the main character of the series in the first eight issues, Gaiman backs up several thousand years to the dawn of humankind, telling the story of Nada, queen of the City of Glass, and her brief love affair with Morpheus. When she refuses to be his queen, he sentences her to Hell, where she spends more than ten thousand years. In a morality play, this act would be narrated by Pride and perhaps some form of Cruelty, and it establishes a core facet of Morpheus's personality. After all, as the storyteller says, "Love is not part of the Dreamworld. Love belongs to Desire, and Desire is always cruel."[28] By falling in love, Morpheus has stepped outside of his function, which never ends well for him. In "A Hope in Hell," before Nada's story is related, Morpheus sees Nada in Hell and refuses to forgive her and set her free. Not until Desire and Death point out to him in no uncertain terms that he has been cruel beyond reason does he begin to work to make things right with Nada.

Morpheus's pride rears its head again in "Men of Good Fortune," in which Morpheus and Death allow a fourteenth-century man to refuse to die. Robert "Hob" Gadling agrees to meet with Morpheus every hundred years to check in. Five hundred years later, Gadling declares that the real reason Morpheus meets with him isn't because he's curious about what happens when a man doesn't die, but because he's lonely and wants a friend. Morpheus's reaction is immediate and violent: "You *dare?* You dare imply that I might befriend a mortal? That one of my kind might *need* companionship? You dare to call me lonely?"[29] Their next meeting is scheduled for 1989, and in a demonstration of Morpheus's ability to change, he attends and refers to Gadling as a friend.[30] Despite his frequent assertions that his status as an anthropomorphic personification means that he is incapable of change, sometime in the twentieth century he begins to recognize his flaws and atone for them.

His atonement involves rescuing Nada from Hell and apologizing to her, then making things right with his son, Orpheus. Unfortunately for him, this means killing Orpheus, who has repeatedly asked for death. Just as in the Greek myth, this Orpheus attempted to rescue his wife, Eurydice, from Hades, but was ripped apart by the maenads—wild women who worship Dionysus, god of wine, fertility, and insanity. In *Sandman,* Orpheus's head remains alive and conscious for centuries because of Morpheus's refusal to kill him. Kinslaying is a violation of divine law, which opens the door for the tripartite goddess in their role as the Furies to punish Morpheus. Thus, Morpheus's death is the result of his own actions and his own choices. He has several opportunities to prevent it, none of which he takes, because each one would mean failing in his duties, breaking his promises, or going against his nature. Finally, as his enemies close in, he turns himself over to Death, refusing to die on anyone else's terms. "I have made all the preparations necessary," he tells her as they meet, alone on a mountaintop.[31] Like Everyman, he has balanced his ledger, and now goes alone to his death, the only way anyone can. "You've been making them for ages," she responds. "You just didn't let yourself know that's what you were doing."[32] Living is preparation for dying, as the roots of this particular death go back to the beginning of the series. Unlike a morality-play everyman, however, Morpheus does not appear to have an afterlife as such. While Everyman and Humanum Genus are afforded a chance for mercy after death, Morpheus ceases to exist. His title passes to a new host, and the story comes to a close.

The strength of *Sandman* as a compelling story is in Morpheus's dual nature as allegory and person, as a flawed protagonist of his own story despite being presented as a narrative device. We are able to identify, or at least empathize, with him, not because he is an everyman but because he is, despite his own protests, fundamentally a person, one transmuted into flesh and blood by Gaiman's skilled manipulation of medieval tropes.

CHAPTER TWO

Crossing the Threshold

Sandman and Medieval Dream Visions

"Do you know what Freud said about dreams of flying?" Rose Walker asks Morpheus as he carries her through the air. "It means you're *really* dreaming about having sex." Morpheus responds, "Tell me, then, what does it mean when you dream about having sex?"[1] Rose doesn't have an answer for this and quickly changes the subject.

Western understanding of what dreams are, where they come from, and what they're for has changed dramatically over the millennia, but for a good stretch of the classical and medieval periods, philosophy discussed whether dreams were revelations from God (or the gods), temptations from demons, or possibly nothing at all. In literature, of course, dreams always have a meaning, constructed as they are by the author for some literary purpose; indeed, in the Middle Ages, dream vision was a major subgenre of poetry in particular.

Medieval dream vision has a robust foundation in classical philosophy. Medieval writers tended to be familiar with Boethius's *Consolation of Philosophy* (c. 524 CE) and Macrobius's *Commentary on "The Dream of Scipio"* (c. 500s CE). *Consolation* is a straightforward allegory, with Philosophy herself visiting Boethius while he's in prison and reminding him that God is fair and just and has a plan. Macrobius's *Commentary* is a robust exploration of various philosophical and scientific beliefs of the time, including a breakdown of a continuum of dreams. He lists five types: enigmatic, prophetic, oracular, nightmare, and apparition. He also includes five varieties of meaning in the enigmatic dreams:

personal, alien, social, public, and universal. Any given dream may fall into multiple categories.[2]

The earliest known formal, structured dream vision poem is *The Romance of the Rose*, written by Guillaume de Lorris around 1225 CE and completed by Jean de Meun around 1269 CE. Generally speaking, the dream is the story of how the dreamer (the Lover) meets and woos his love, represented by a rose. Much like the morality plays discussed in chapter 1, *The Romance of the Rose* is chock-full of allegorical figures like Pleasure, Shame, Chastity, Fair Welcome, and Evil Tongue. Throughout the poem, the Lover is lectured to about love, life, philosophy, death, and living well. Other dream visions followed throughout the next few hundred years, with Geoffrey Chaucer himself writing at least six.

Because dream visions were used for so many purposes and over such a long span of time, it's nearly impossible to make sweeping statements about what they were for, but generally they were didactic. Considering their roots in philosophy, this is hardly surprising. All Guillaume de Lorris and Jean de Meun did was bring in tropes of chivalric romance, opening up the scope of dream vision but not fundamentally changing its tendency toward preachiness. Dream visions could be religious or secular, long or short, clear or opaque with their messages.

Dream-interpretation methods have changed a lot over the course of human history, but we're still looking for meaning in them. Dream visions were one literary method of exploring how dreams could impart higher knowledge—or, in some cases, parody the idea that they could. *Sandman* is a great big exploration of dreams and dreaming, so it's no surprise that it would draw on medieval dream visions as one method of telling its story. In the Sandman universe, dreams can be nonsense—just our sleeping minds spitting out images—or they can be a method through which the universe makes itself known. The series contains several important, story-defining dreams that share several structural features with dream vision as it was used in medieval poetry.

....

ROSE WALKER, THE VORTEX OF DREAM

Rose Walker comes to prominence in the *Sandman* narrative in *The Doll's House* arc. Before she even appears on page, we're told that a "dream vortex" is coming, and that somehow she will factor into Desire's latest attempt to bring down Morpheus.[3] While we are not immediately told what a dream vortex is, we see some of her abilities almost at once; she falls asleep and makes her way into the Dreaming. She watches Lucien warn Morpheus about several missing dreams and the rumors that a vortex has arisen. Morpheus says he knows about the vortex and points to Rose's viewpoint in the corner of the throne room.[4] The Netflix series allows Rose more agency; she physically walks through Morpheus's palace and speaks directly to him rather than being relegated to a fly-on-the-wall viewpoint.[5]

Both Rose and Morpheus have missing people or dreams to find, though, so the dream vortex issue is put aside until the end of the arc. When it arises again, however, it is striking how well Rose's experience matches up with the structure of a medieval dream vision. After a traumatic experience that culminates in finding her missing, abused brother, Rose returns to the boarding house where she's been staying. The encounter that follows is nearly beat for beat a dream vision in the medieval sense, falling into the "oracular" and "universal" classifications in Macrobius's taxonomy of dreams. Namely, a guide arrives to advise Rose and warn her that something will happen to the universe if action isn't taken.

Rose is upset about her brother and everything she's been through in the last few weeks, and this mental and emotional turmoil is preventing her from sleeping. Dreamers experiencing some sort of distress, concern, or problem that keeps them awake is a frequent opening frame for a dream vision. Chaucer's narrator of *The Book of the Duchess* is sleeping so badly he's amazed he's still alive; he has "so many an ydel thoght" and thinks "I hold hit be a sicknesse/That I have suffred this eight yeere."[6] The narrator of "Pearl" is upset by the loss of his pearl (most frequently read to mean his daughter); in his grief, he goes to the garden where the pearl was lost and is struck down into "a slepyng-slaȝte," or deathlike sleep.[7] For the narrator of William Langland's *Piers Plowman*, sleep comes more quickly, but he is also "unholy of werkes."[8] In captions representing Rose's thoughts, she reminds the reader that "in the last three weeks I'd found an unknown grandmother and a long-lost brother. Now it looked like I might lose both of them."[9] She's tired, but she's worried and can't sleep, even as everyone who shares her boarding house falls asleep and dreams.

Their dreams are mostly nonsense, born of latent desires and fears. Only when Rose finally falls asleep does everything go sideways. This brings us to the second part of a dream vision: the dream itself—or, as literary critic Stephen J. Russell calls it, the dream report.[10] This is the meat of a dream vision poem or story—the part where everything happens and the lesson is taught. It is invariably the *longest* part of a dream poem, and the part most packed with meaning.

The dream part of a dream vision is usually heavily allegorical; embodied virtues, vices, gods, goddesses, and ideas appear to make their cases and impart the lesson of the dream to the dreamer. In *The Romance of the Rose*, the Lover is taught how to woo his lady and circumvent obstacles such as Shame and Evil Tongue. In "Pearl," the dreamer's lost daughter appears to him and lectures him about God and the afterlife. Chaucer's *Parliament of Foules* examines societal hierarchies through the love lives of birds. In Rose's case, she's whisked out of her destructive dream vortexing by Morpheus, the anthropomorphic personification of dreaming itself. In dream visions, flying is often used as a metaphor for understanding—that is, for gaining knowledge that brings one closer to God.[11] Morpheus imparts this higher knowledge to Rose.

He explains to her that she is a dream vortex, and this means she must die. Rose moves from anger to denial to acceptance, but then she insists that this is only a dream; she'll wake up eventually and be safe. Like most dream vision protagonists, she fails to immediately grasp the lesson she's being taught. However, because she's a modern dream vision protagonist, her difficulties are different than a medieval dream vision protagonist. Rose has a modern idea of what dreams are. She does not consider them true visions sent by a spiritual power but rather fundamentally false images coming from her own psyche. She invokes Freud, who notoriously turned every symbol into something sexual, only for Morpheus to call that method of dream interpretation into question.

The landscape of a dream vision is also important; gardens and other such locations are almost universally the setting for medieval dream visions. *The Romance of the Rose* takes place in a garden described as paradise, full of trees, flowers, and birds. The narrator of "Pearl" describes a dream landscape comprising a forest full of crystal cliffs, enormous trees, and pearlescent gravel.[12] Chaucer's *Parliament of Foules* narrator enters a lush garden, and his *House of Fame* narrator is in the temple of Venus. However it manifests, the dream vision setting represents an idealized, heavenly landscape, usually based on the Garden of Eden.[13]

In Rose's case, she is not merely dreaming. She has been physically transported to a location within the Dreaming. At first that location is brown, rocky, and desolate because the place that is supposed to be there is missing, and also because Rose isn't here for consolation or love but instead to be killed. Gaiman inverts the usual dream garden landscape to represent the threat to Rose. The landscape arrives a bit later in the form of Gilbert, the human version of a place, Fiddler's Green—traditionally where sailors go when they die, and thus a heavenly location. Gilbert's arrival marks a shift in the dream's trajectory; as he ceases to appear human and becomes a garden again, the vision becomes more traditional, more of a consolation—because Rose's grandmother arrives and convinces Morpheus not to kill Rose. Instead, he sends her back to the world.

Waking is a necessary step in a dream vision poem, but they rarely end there. After all, a dream vision was an answer to a problem the dreamer was struggling with, and that problem must be reconsidered in light of the dream. The final structural part of the medieval dream vision is the epilogue, "describing the reawakening of the dreamer and occasionally offering interpretive comments on the dream report."[14] The epilogues of dream visions are of varying lengths and levels of detail; *The Romance of the Rose* doesn't have one at all, ending when the Lover is allowed to pluck his rose and "scatter a little seed."[15] *The Book of the Duchess* narrator's main problem was an inability to sleep, so his epilogue is only a few lines in which he notes that he had a weird dream and plans to write it down.[16] In *Parliament of Foules*, the narrator is tired of serving love and is reading Scipio, trying to learn "a certeyn thing."[17] He wakes still unsatisfied and determines to read more from different books. The "Pearl" narrator relinquishes his pearl/daughter to God, the dream having served as solace for his grief over her loss. The *Piers Plowman* epilogue is much longer, containing a discussion of how dreams cannot usually be trusted, though there are stories in the Bible that explain circumstances in which they can be, and how his dream's lesson warns people not to buy their pardons because only good deeds can get one into Heaven.[18] Dreamers each spend time analyzing their dream and, if necessary, interpreting it.

For Rose, the epilogue is a lengthy journal entry in which she grapples with her reaction to her dream. Having been given a glimpse of the metaphysical structure of Gaiman's Sandman universe, Rose is rendered helpless, terrified, and paralyzed rather than illuminated or consoled: "If my dream was true," she writes, "then everything we know, everything we think we know, is a lie."[19] In order to move on, she has to set the dream aside—to classify it, per Macrobius, as a nightmare, having no meaning and not worth brooding over. Only then is she able to pull herself out of her depression and rejoin her newly reunited family.

....

JED WALKER'S NIGHTMARES

Rose isn't the only one to dream in *The Doll's House*; nor are her housemates. While Rose's dreams are true dreams and her housemates' dreams are regular psychological dreams, there's one more character having dreams that fit neither mold. Jed Walker, Rose's brother, lives in the grip of the type of dream Macrobius would classify as an apparition, brought on by demons and occurring in the half-waking state just before falling asleep. These aren't true dreams, like Rose's dream, but actively harmful dreams brought on by demons.

Jed's dreams are inflicted on him by a pair of nightmares named Brute and Glob. Their goal is to create a whole new Dreaming with themselves as its rulers, using Jed's mind, the ghost of Hector Hall (the Golden Age Sandman), and Hector's wife, Lyta. Brute and Glob represent evil, or at least vice—forces that would prevent people from reaching the truth. They hold Jed's mind captive for two years before the events of *The Doll's House*.[20]

In contrast to Rose's hyperrealistic dreams that show her higher truths about the universe, Jed's dreams are extremely simplistic, borrowing heavily from the story and art style of the 1910s to 1920s comic strip *Little Nemo in Slumberland* by Winsor McKay.[21] In the first dream we see on page, Jed is flying with Hector and Lyta, but rather than flight representing an ascent to higher knowledge, he falls.[22] He sleeps to escape, but cut off from the Dreaming, his sleep doesn't have the psychologically restorative properties usually brought on by dreams.

Jed's mind becomes a battlefield as Morpheus fights his way in to free him from Brute and Glob. Hector attempts to fight back, still believing himself the hero and Morpheus an enormous nightmare monster, but he can't stand up to the real Sandman. Morpheus frees Jed and sends Brute and Glob to the darkness. Jed's dreams establish a bit more of the metaphysical structure of dreams and Morpheus's dominion over them. Just as classical and medieval philosophy warned against dreams sent by demons, Jed's dreams are an aberration, an affront to Morpheus's authority, just as demonic dreams would be an affront to God's. Brute and Glob lead Jed, Hector, and Lyta astray, thus bringing down the wrath of a being of immeasurable power.

DANIEL HALL VISITS THE DREAMING

Lyta Hall, Hector's wife, appears again in "The Parliament of Rooks," the title of which clearly references Chaucer's *Parliament of Foules,* which adds another layer of intention to the dream vision nature of the issue.[23] As her son, Daniel, naps, he travels into the Dreaming and meets with several well-known residents. This is foreshadowing for Daniel's eventual role as Dream; his dream is true and interactive. Not even Rose's dream of Morpheus's palace allowed her to appear fully corporeal and talk to and touch the denizens of the Dreaming. Daniel, who gestated for two years in a world resembling the Dreaming and will take over as Dream after Morpheus's death, is much more attuned to dreams and dreaming, so his interaction with the Dreaming and its inhabitants is different than anyone else's.

Daniel's dream follows the structure of dream visions as detailed above, though his prologue and epilogue belong more to Lyta than they do to him, probably because of his youth and mostly preverbal developmental stage. Lyta complains to a friend about her lack of adult interaction while Daniel falls asleep in his crib. She also notes that he's growing up and getting into things, commenting, "It won't be long before he figures out how to get out of his crib."[24] In the nursery, Daniel is indeed getting out of his crib, though the artwork is unclear about whether he's dreaming or actually climbing out. The line between sleeping and dreaming is much blurrier for Daniel than for any other character.

The transition from sleeping to dreaming (or his movement from earth to the Dreaming) is more pronounced than in Rose's dreams

Baby Daniel crawls from his nursery to the Dreaming (*Sandman* 40).

as well. One panel shows an entire wall of Daniel's nursery; the wall is painted with the alphabet and several animals, and his changing table and a trash can line the right wall. Daniel moves past the changing table, and the perpendicular wall disappears while the back wall continues. The alphabet also continues on past Z into non-English symbols and letters, and the floor turns into dirt and rock rather than carpet. This is where he encounters Gregory the gargoyle, which establishes for the reader that he's in the Dreaming.

Unlike most dream vision narrators, Daniel doesn't require a guide. He collects companions as he travels—Gregory, Matthew (a raven), and Eve—but none of them is interested in teaching him anything or guiding him anywhere. Yet his dream is still populated by allegories and metaphors, most notably Eve, Cain, and Abel, who, on the surface, are characters from Genesis or Bereishit. Like Morpheus, they are real and not real; Matthew asks how literal their existence is as it relates to the Bible, and Abel starts to explain that none of their stories happened on earth before Cain shuts him up.[25] But when Eve tries to avoid telling a story by saying she doesn't do that anymore, Cain says that "storytellers who don't tell stories aren't anything. They're nothing at all."[26] Like Morpheus, they are what they do; their fundamental role provides their raison d'être.

At this point, Daniel ceases being the focal point of the story as Cain, Abel, Eve, and Matthew squabble and have tea. The lack of a single, purposeful guide doesn't mean that Daniel isn't exposed to higher knowledge, though he doesn't yet have the cognitive ability to understand it. Because he isn't able to ask the questions and take in the lessons that a dream vision narrator usually would, Matthew takes up the role of the ignorant, questioning character. Cain tells Matthew about the mystery of the parliament of rooks; Eve tells everyone about Adam beginning as an androgyne giant split in two and his three wives—Lilith, a nameless one, and Eve; and Abel tells the story about how Cain killed him, and Death and Dream brought him into the Dreaming to be the keeper of the House of Secrets. Only when Cain decides the fun is over and kicks everyone out does Daniel take center stage again. Eve carries him outside, sending him back to the waking world.

The epilogue of Daniel's dream returns to Lyta, who finds a black feather—probably one of Matthew's—in his crib. She discards it as trash, but it adds to the mystery of just how physical Daniel's visit to the Dreaming was. Daniel is too young to understand yet, but his dream introduces him to the major players in the Dreaming and exposes him to some of the core functions and rules of the Dreaming. When Morpheus dies and Daniel takes over as Dream, these players will help him settle in and decide what kind of Dream he wants to be.

In each case of true dreaming in *Sandman*, Gaiman follows the structure of the medieval dream vision, both in plot points and in their use as teaching tools for character development. His use of dream vision shows familiarity with the classical and medieval philosophies around dreams and dreaming—from the gates of horn and ivory to the lesson that appears specific to the dreamer but can be generalized to the reader. He uses the traditional dream vision structure to explore the nature of dreams, humanity, and the metaphysical makeup of the Sandman universe, all while moving the plot and characters forward.

CHAPTER THREE

Abandon Hope

Sandman Goes to Hell

Theories about the afterlife are a mainstay of human religion (or lack of religion), and medieval Christianity was positively obsessed with it. Probably the most influential work on the nature of the Christian afterlife comes from Dante Alighieri (c. 1265–1321 CE) and his *Divine Comedy* (1320 CE). Drawing heavily on Roman Catholicism, Aristotle's *Ethics*, the Franciscans and Dominicans, and Boethius's *Consolation of Philosophy*, as well as his own life experience, Dante constructed what has come to be the single most popular understanding of the structure of Hell.[1]

When Gaiman sends Morpheus to Hell in issue 4, "A Hope in Hell," and early in the *Season of Mists* arc (the third major story arc, issues 21–28), he uses his usual intertextual approach to explore and interrogate various philosophies, but especially Christian philosophy as expressed by Dante and John Milton. As familiar as *Inferno* and *Paradise Lost* are to most readers, having seeped into the zeitgeist through repeated use and retelling, these texts serve as a shorthand for Gaiman to invite readers in. This is how medievalism works in many cases; we have ideas about how the Middle Ages were or looked based on other pop-cultural texts, and certain touchstones, like castles, knights, and barbarians, serve to evoke a medieval milieu. For these issues, Gaiman blends Dante's circular geography of Hell with Milton's well-spoken and charismatic Lucifer to create a foundation for readers before launching into deeper thematic explorations. However, he does not allow these familiar traditions to restrict him; they illuminate, rather than define, his world building. Full recognition and understanding of his literary antecedents aren't necessary for the reader, though they do add depth and resonance for those readers who recognize them.

FINDING HOPE IN HELL

In this first visit to Hell, Gaiman uses Dante's *Inferno* mostly as a shorthand to introduce us to the concept of Hell as it exists in the DC Comics/Sandman universe. *Inferno* is a convenient text to borrow from because it's so baked into popular ideas about Hell that even people who haven't actually read it will recognize the geography of the circles, and probably the Wood of Suicides and City of Dis. However, Gaiman's compost heap approach means that he doesn't lock himself into a strictly Dantean idea of the construction of Hell. He uses only what he needs for the story, bringing in other texts such as *Paradise Lost* or making up things entirely.

Gaiman telegraphs his influences from Dante from the very beginning of "A Hope in Hell," in which Morpheus goes to Hell seeking his helmet, which was stolen and sold while he was imprisoned. The cover of the issue, painted by Dave McKean, features Lucifer staring at the reader. Across the lower half of his face and chest are lines 56–84 from canto 34 of *Inferno*—the part where Virgil explains to Dante that the three heads of Lucifer are chewing on Judas Iscariot, Brutus, and Cassius, then carries Dante out of Hell by climbing down Lucifer's back. Lucifer is framed by burned pages from the *Purgatorio*, the second part of Dante's *Divine Comedy*, in which Beatrice leads Dante through Purgatory. For readers paying close attention, the invocation of Dante's version of Hell is evident before they even start reading the issue. Yet the difference is evident as well; this Lucifer has one head and is blond and beautiful, not the three-headed monstrosity of *Inferno*.

The cover of *Sandman* 4 anticipates the Dantean elements of its story line.

Morpheus begins his journey in a nowhere between worlds, alone. Unlike Dante, who is rescued from being lost in a dark wood by Virgil, Morpheus finds his own way to the gates of Hell. The gates themselves are more grotesque than Dante's, which consist only of a portal with the well-known inscription above them:

Through me you pass into the city of woe;
Through me you pass into eternal pain;
Through me among the people lost for aye.
Justice the founder of my fabric moved:
To rear me was the task of power divine,
Supremest wisdom and primeval love.
Before me things create were none, save things
Eternal, and eternal I endure.
All hope abandon, ye who enter here.[2]

No such inscription appears in *Sandman*, yet the idea of hope and Hell being antitheses still comes through. Morpheus, in his internal monologue, notes that he "do[es] not have high hopes for this meeting," but he *does* have hope, and it is the concept of hope that he later uses as a weapon against the demon Choronzon and Hell as a whole.[3] The physical gates are built of stone and twisted human bodies; Klinger compares them to Auguste Rodin's sculpture "The Gates of Hell."[4]

Morpheus is allowed past the gates by a demon named Squatterbloat, a silly name that echoes the ones Dante gave his demons: Graffiacane, Cagnazzo, Barbariccia, and Malacoda (translated by Michael Palma as Scratchbitch, Baddog, Spikebeard, and Wickedtail).[5] Dante's demons talk to each other much the way the evil influences of the morality plays do: with a lack of respect and a lot of scatological humor and insults. Getting past Squatterbloat is the first of Morpheus's tests to prove his strength and ability to face down Lucifer and the demonic hordes. But the demon who takes Morpheus from the gates to see Lucifer is Etrigan, a Jack Kirby creation who alternately clashed with and fought beside DC Comics heroes such as Batman. Etrigan serves as a guide, as Virgil does for Dante, through the circles of Hell.

The geographical markers for Hell that Gaiman provides here are about three-quarters Dantean and one-quarter uniquely Gaimanian. Unlike other visitors to Hell in various visionary epics, Morpheus only sees a small fraction of it in this issue, so it's worth exploring where he visits and why. What is it about these particular locales that Gaiman wants us to see, know, understand, or associate with Morpheus himself? In medieval visionary literature, the dreamer/pilgrim is shown things directly relevant to personal circumstances. Often the pilgrims are in danger of being trapped in Hell, especially while passing through areas that punish sins they're guilty of. In "A Hope in Hell," Morpheus isn't here (initially) to be warned about his fate or taught about the afterlife; he is, after all, Endless and undying. He doesn't have to worry about Hell. Instead, he's here to rectify a wrong done to him when he was kidnapped, imprisoned, and robbed. But Hell isn't a place that would let a chance like this go to waste, so the places Etrigan drags Morpheus through are directly relevant to his story.

Once past the gates, the first recognizable landmark is the Wood of Suicides. Like Dante, Morpheus breaks a twig from one of the branches, which allows the soul trapped inside the tree to speak; it talks about how its life had become unbearable, "all too much. Sandra knew everything. And the papers. So I had to."[6] It thought suicide would make the pain stop, but as the chorus of "hurt, hurting, hurting, hurt" from the forest attests, it didn't.[7] This could be foreshadowing Morpheus's death; he too becomes overwhelmed and trapped by his choices and his responsibilities, choosing to die on his own terms rather than allowing the Furies to destroy him. Morpheus also notes that the wood is larger than he remembers; his takeaway is that Hell is changing.[8] Lani Diane Rich and Alisa Kwitney speculate that the reason the Wood is larger than his last visit is because of his imprisonment; with Morpheus gone, people didn't have dreams, stories, or hope the way they ought, and more people may have died by suicide as a result.[9] In a few pages, Morpheus will learn just how much Hell has changed.

Weep-Not, a cliff face full of prison cells, is the next stop, and this is where we meet Nada for the first time. She peers between the bars, hoping that Morpheus—known as Kai'ckul in her culture—has come to free her at last, after ten thousand years of imprisonment. He has not. The encounter lasts only a page, eight panels, but it carries multiple layers of meaning and implication. At the surface level, Morpheus encounters a woman he loves who rejected him, and whose rejection he reacted to by sentencing her to Hell. He says he still loves her but has not forgiven her, which is appropriate for Hell—a place where there is no hope of forgiveness.[10]

When we learn Nada's story, we discover that she rejected him because it's against the rules of the universe for a mortal to love an Endless. When she does finally give in and have sex with him, the sun destroys her city with a fireball, killing everyone. She does everything she can think of to escape him and prevent yet more destruction, including jumping off a cliff to her death. But because Morpheus is Endless, that doesn't stop him. He asks her twice more to be his queen. She refuses, and he condemns her to eternal torment.[11]

So her placement in Hell is curious. She is not in the Wood of Suicides, which would make the most sense. Instead, she's in an area Gaiman invented called Weep-Not, possibly because her only crime (if it can be considered one) was injuring Morpheus's pride.[12] She did nothing to earn a place in any of the nine circles of Dante's Hell; even her suicide wasn't the violence-against-self act that is punished in the Wood of Suicides but rather an attempt to protect the world from the consequences of her love for Morpheus. In *Season of Mists,* the reasons people end up in Hell are explicated further, but it is made clear that Nada is here because Morpheus is angry with her. Morpheus asks why Etrigan led him this way, but Hell is about torturing people to punish sin, and forcing Morpheus to face his own sin is well in line with a demon's idea of fun.

Finally, Etrigan leads Morpheus to the City of Dis, the great city of Hell that contains the eighth and ninth circles and where the fallen angels live. In *Inferno,* Dante is deliberately delayed at the gates, taunted by the Furies (Megaera, Alecto, and Tisphone), and threatened with the arrival of Medusa before an angel arrives demanding that Virgil and Dante be allowed through the gates. This is the only place in *Inferno* where there's a direct and serious threat to Dante's safety. Morpheus doesn't face the Furies or any aspect of them here, but they are a constant presence throughout his story and ultimately the last threat to his life.

Although the basic structure of Hell in this issue follows some plot beats from Dante, Gaiman's Lucifer is Miltonian. Modeled on a young David Bowie, Lucifer is beautiful, androgynous, and *not* frozen in ice up to his middle, with three heads chomping on traitors.[13] This makes sense: a Lucifer who doesn't talk wouldn't be very interesting for the story. Hell does have three rulers, however, thanks to DC Comics' *Crisis on Infinite Earths*;[14] Azazel and Beelzebub have joined Lucifer in a triumvirate. Thus, the portrayal of Lucifer is an interesting blend of Milton's Satan and a pop-culture idea of agender androgyny, adjusted to fit the continuity of the greater DC Comics universe. In the Netflix series, the triumvirate was dropped, returning the focus to Lucifer themself[15] and easing closer to the Miltonian idea of the ruler of Hell. In fact, many of the direct references and links to the DC Comics universe were dropped or muted, partially because, as Gaiman puts it, "no human being watching this should actually be obligated to understand 1989 DC Comics continuity in order to make sense of this."[16]

MORPHEUS, LUCIFER, MILTON, AND DANTE

Morpheus returns to Hell nineteen issues later in "Season of Mists: Episode 2" (issue 23). This visit is much different, both because Hell is now empty and because Gaiman has moved away from overt Dantean references and into overt Miltonian references. Although Milton wasn't a medieval writer, and *Paradise Lost* was influenced by Homer, Virgil, and the Bible far more than medieval romance or epics, Milton is such an enormous and obvious influence here that ignoring him entirely would be to miss a good bit of the point of the arc. Likewise, medievalism has a tendency to incorporate elements from both earlier and later historical periods (such as Rome or the Tudors) into its understanding of "the medieval," so even though Milton isn't strictly medieval, he can still be considered in a medievalist analysis of *Sandman*. But Gaiman's emphasis on Milton at this point doesn't mean that the Dantean undertones and thematic influences are completely gone. Gaiman has again pulled from his compost heap to create a version of Hell that contains enough obvious references to major precursors that they serve as a shorthand.

Before departing for Hell, Morpheus sends Cain as an envoy to warn Lucifer of his visit; sometime between "A Hope in Hell" and "Season of Mists: Episode 1," Lucifer has retaken complete control of Hell. He brags to Cain that there is only one greater than him, "and to Him . . . to Him we no longer speak."[17] He follows this with a direct quote from Milton: "Better to reign in Hell, than to serve in Heaven."[18] But he also immediately acknowledges the provenance of the quote and then rejects it, pointing out that Milton was blind, both literally and metaphorically. Literary critics Joakim Jahlmar, Noelle Leslie dela Cruz, and Adam Porter analyze how Milton and *Paradise Lost* are reflected and rejected in *A Season of Mists*, including ideas regarding sin and punishment, free will and determinism.[19] The parallels are obvious because they're meant to be. *A Season of Mists* is almost in direct conversation with *Paradise Lost*—but not exclusively.

In "Season of Mists: Episode 2," Morpheus once again enters Hell. Unlike his first visit, he goes to Hell in order to right a wrong that he has committed, rather than to address one committed against him. He briefly considers not going at all, instead staying in the void between dimensions. Then he thinks, "NO. We do as we must do."[20] This statement is not dissimilar to one repeated in *Inferno:* "So 'tis will'd / Where will and power are one."[21] Virgil uses this statement first to get Dante past Charon and into Hell, and again to get him past Minos. His argument is that it is Dante's destiny to make this journey, and therefore the lords of Hell cannot and should not stand in his way. Similarly, Destiny himself put Morpheus in a position to realize that he needed to atone for his treatment of Nada, and hiding between worlds—essentially dying—will not accomplish that task.

Morpheus enters Hell unopposed and unremarked, but he finds Nada's cell—and indeed all of Hell—completely empty. Lucifer appears and explains that he has quit: "I've *stopped.* I've *resigned.* I'm *leaving.* Can I make myself any clearer?"[22] He invites Morpheus to join him as he kicks out the last few souls and demons and locks up. Morpheus thus embarks on a larger tour of Hell, this time with Lucifer himself as his guide. Literary critic Zainab Younus points out that while Dante was guided through a full Hell and talks to the inmates, Morpheus is guided through an empty Hell.[23] He does encounter one soul—Breschau of Livonia—who allows Lucifer to obliquely question the justice of eternal punishment, but Morpheus isn't here to learn about sin and punishment. He is here to be shown that it is possible to cease being the king of his realm—to simply refuse and give it all up. Instead of spending time with mortal souls, Morpheus spends time with Lucifer and listens to his story and complaints.

The importance of stories to earthly immortality is a core theme of *Inferno;* Dante spends a lot of time asking for souls' stories so he can remind the living of their existence. One of Morpheus's titles is Prince of Stories, linking him to a similar idea. However, unlike Dante, Morpheus learns only two stories in Hell, Lucifer's and Breschau's. Breschau is an example of how a lack of stories leads to true death. He lists his sins—a litany of rape, murder, torture, and mutilation. He claims that this is his just punishment and refuses to leave Hell. Lucifer tells him that he's been here for 1,100 years, nobody remembers him, and few even remember where Livonia was. The people he hurt are dead and gone, as are their children and their children's children. He made no lasting mark on the world. This contrasts with Lucifer's story: Lucifer's rebellion is billions of years old, yet the world is still aware of it, and Lucifer spends the whole issue explaining himself to Morpheus, airing his grievances. The characters in *Inferno* and "Season of Mists: Episode 2" want to be remembered on their own terms, which requires others hearing and passing along their stories.

THEMES AND PARALLELS

Thematically as well as textually, *Season of Mists* shares a great deal with both *Inferno* and *Paradise Lost* in a way that pulls all three into conversation with each other, especially for readers who are familiar with the older texts. The textual parallels are clear enough that the thematic parallels can't be seen as anything but purposeful; Gaiman examines several of the same existential human questions that Milton and Dante did, just through a different lens.

All three texts contain questions about free will. If destiny exists, if God knows everything, how are his creations truly free? In Morpheus's case, the issue is Destiny and his book and Morpheus's own sense of responsibility. Lucien, librarian of the Dreaming and one of Morpheus's closest advisors, suggests that Morpheus doesn't have to go to Hell at all, but Morpheus responds: "We do what we must, Lucien. Sometimes we can choose the path we follow. Sometimes our choices are made for us. And sometimes we have no choice at all."[24] Yet even if destiny/Destiny already knows or determines our paths, we are still responsible for our choices. Lucifer rejects the idea (which Milton embraced) that he has anything to do with human sin; people just want someone to blame, he claims, and then someone to punish them for their transgressions when they die.[25] People are in Hell because they want to be, not because someone sent them. He also questions just how free *he* was in his rebellion: "I still wonder how much of it was planned. How much of it He knew in advance. I thought I was *rebelling*. I thought I was *defying* His rule. No. . . . I was merely fulfilling another tiny segment of *His* great and powerful plan."[26] Dante also emphasizes how one's own choices result in damnation. He divides Hell into three categories of sin: incontinence, violence, and fraudulence. The lower circles of Hell are reserved for the fraudulent because the sins punished there—pandering, thievery, forgery, and treachery—require more purpose and forethought than lust or gluttony, which are sins of incontinence (lack of self-control), and suicide or murder, which are sins of violence (rage, passion, despair). Intent matters for Dante, though as a whole, sinners have nobody to blame but themselves for winding up where they are.

All three also discuss the concept of divine justice. Dante builds a Hell where the punishment fits the sin; the torture mirrors the fundamental nature of the action that caused a soul's damnation. Gaiman's Lucifer, like Milton's Satan, questions whether eternal punishment—especially for actions God knew someone would take—is truly just. "Yes, I rebelled," Lucifer says. "It was a long time ago. How long was I meant to pay for that one action?"[27] *Forever*, reply Milton and Dante. Unlike Purgatory, there's no escaping Hell. Gaiman pushes back against forever; Lucifer quits, and the angel Remiel declares that no longer will Hell be a place of mindless, purposeless punishment but instead a place of redemption.[28] In this way it becomes more like Purgatory, which does not seem to exist in the DC Comics/Sandman universe as it does in the Catholic idea of the afterlife; only Hell and the Silver City (which is not Heaven but is where the angels live) are confirmed as existing in this mythos. Porter also compares this new version of Hell to the Jewish Gehenna, pointing out the many parallels between the way Gaiman writes Hell and Lucifer and the stories of the Aggadic Midrash.[29] In this theology, most souls go to Gehenna only for a short time—about a year—with eternal punishment reserved for the very worst.

The order of the universe and its hierarchy is another common theme that also serves to illustrate Morpheus's priorities. Dante's Hell is purposefully structured, as is Purgatory and Heaven in the rest of the *Divine Comedy*; the mountain of Purgatory is the reflection of the pit of Hell. Gaiman's Lucifer says that Hell is Heaven's opposite, its reflection.[30] Milton argues that Lucifer's true crime, the core of his rebellion, was rejecting God's elevation of the Son and thus the divine order of the universe. When Lucifer empties Hell, it throws the world into chaos, with the dead returning to earth and Death scrambling to right the natural order. Remember that Morpheus's main personality trait is a stubborn insistence on duty, responsibility, and order. When handed the key to Hell, he never considers keeping it; Hell, after all, is not under the auspices of Dream. Instead, after petitions from representatives of various pantheons, Faerie, and evicted demons, he returns Hell to Heaven's oversight, under the supervision of the angels Remiel and Duma. As God, speaking through Remiel, says: "Hell is Heaven's reflection. It is Heaven's shadow. They define each other. Reward and Punishment; hope and despair. There must be a Hell, for without Hell, Heaven has no meaning."[31] While Morpheus was uncertain regarding every other request for the key to Hell put to him, this one has him turning over the key immediately and without question. Rather than an overhaul of the universe's structure, he allows it to stand as it always has, with Hell part of the Christian order, under the rule of angels, punishing sinners.

Gaiman's allusions to and conversation with arguably the two most influential texts on Lucifer and Hell lay a foundation for his own arguments about the nature of evil, the afterlife, and human nature. Some of these ideas align with Dante and Milton, while others seem to come from Gaiman's Jewish upbringing. By using *Paradise Lost* and *Inferno* as foundational works, Gaiman off-loads much of the world building, which allows him to take up less narrative space in the comic itself and makes it clear that these debates are ongoing human concerns. These explorations are also instrumental in revealing aspects of Morpheus's character, especially his strict belief in duty and the order of the universe, which are central to his narrative arc and his ultimate death.

CHAPTER FOUR

The Wizard Tim

The Books of Magic

In December 1990–March 1991, about the same time early issues of *Season of Mists* were coming out, DC Comics also published *The Books of Magic,* a four-part story written by Gaiman that pulled together most of the magical characters of the DC Comics universe and introduced a new one: Timothy Hunter. In addition to integrating it with DC Comics continuity with characters like John Constantine, Doctor Occult, Mister E, and the Phantom Stranger, *The Books of Magic* also includes journeys into the Dreaming and Faerie as they appear in *Sandman. The Books of Magic* includes many of the same themes and motifs as *Sandman,* as well as echoing a great deal of *Sandman*'s medievalism.

In *The Books of Magic,* twelve-year-old Timothy Hunter comes to the attention of a group of DC Comics magicians dubbed the Trenchcoat Brigade. Concerned about his potential to be an incredibly powerful and possibly evil wizard, they each take him on a journey to show him what magic is and to help him decide whether he wants to be involved with magic at all. While most of the guides (with the exception of Constantine) express a belief in a binary universe—science or magic, fantasy or reality, in or out—Gaiman's narrative view, as literary critic Andrew Eichel argues, is more ambivalent.[1] Both are possible, both are necessary, and black-and-white views of the world are not only overly simplistic but also extremist. The plot structure shows clear parallels to both Joseph Campbell's hero's journey and to other magical-apprenticeship stories, but with obvious differences, most notably that Tim's guides are biased and flawed, and one of them tries to kill him.[2]

The Books of Magic, like many fantasy texts, is heavily medievalist partly because magic is frequently associated with the fantasy Middle Ages. If a modern setting is involved, magic is over, or it has gone underground; science eclipsed it and drove it away. Medievalist Kim Selling explains that the Middle Ages are seen as a time of high fantasy partly because of the romances, which were rife with magic and fantastic creatures, and partly because the era is familiar enough but far enough away that it's easy to believe fantastic things happened there and then.[3] However, the core of Gaiman's argument in *The Books of Magic* is that science and magic are not opposites, despite what Tim's guides keep telling him. Besides a general medievalist aesthetic, Gaiman also draws on medieval texts such as dream visions and Arthuriana, rooting some of Tim's adventure in medieval mythology.

DREAM VISIONING INTO FAERIE

As I discussed in chapter 2, medieval dream visions had a fairly consistent structure and intention. Dreamers are meant to learn a lesson or see something that reconciles a problem they've been having in their waking life. They fall asleep, sometimes crossing a boundary, and a guide takes them through a landscape full of metaphor and allegory—and sometimes danger—while dreamers struggle with the lessons they're being taught. Eventually they wake up and integrate their new knowledge with their lived reality.

By the time Doctor Occult, one of the Trenchcoat Brigade magicians, takes Tim to Faerie, he's already been through a lot, putting him in the usual troubled headspace of a dream vision protagonist. This is his third journey with his fourth guide, he hasn't slept in several days, and his life has constantly been in danger. He's begun to doubt he should have agreed to travel with the Trenchcoat Brigade at all. While no clear falling-asleep point is evident in their journey into Faerie, there are suggestions that Tim might be asleep and dreaming. Crossing the fence between earth and Faerie at twilight is one of them; at another, Doctor Occult says on some level they're sitting on a hillside "exploring a world within ourselves."[4] At the end, Tim wakes up outside the boundaries of Faerie without traveling back the way he came.

Doctor Occult serves as Tim's guide—sort of. As they go through the fence, he changes into a woman, much to Tim's confusion. She has Tim pick a name for her, and he chooses Rose, which she accepts. In the DC Comics mythos, Rose Psychic is Doctor Occult's sidekick/partner (and completely unrelated to Rose Walker), but the parallel to *The Romance of the Rose* is also evident. Tim chooses her name from a nearby rosebush, which he doesn't touch, unlike the Lover of the medieval poem, hinting that Tim is still too young for even metaphorical sexual interest. Their journey through Faerie is episodic, not unlike Dante's journey through Hell.[5] Like the journey in *Inferno,* there is only one road, and it takes Rose and Tim through discrete locations and encounters.

Their first stop is the Goblin Market, a Faerie locale based on Christina Rossetti's poem of the same name. They continue to follow the road, encountering obstacles and dangers. At each one, Tim learns something about Faerie, about magic and being part of a magical community, or both. At last Tim meets Queen Titania, who explains why his journey into fundamentally fictional worlds[6] is so important: "These worlds provide an alternative. Provide an escape. Provide a threat. Provide a dream, and power, provide refuge, and pain. They give your world meaning. They do not exist, and thus they are all that matters."[7] Eichel claims that Titania's speech is an example of how Gaiman's narrative nudges Tim (and the reader) toward understanding that magic and science aren't binaries. Rather, a connected view of fantasy and reality is necessary for full perception and understanding of the world.[8]

FAERIE, HELL, AND ARTHURIANA

One of the major encounters in Faerie involves several medieval mythologies blended together, all loosely linked by Arthurian legend. Arthuriana is the term used to refer to the broad, sprawling collection of interconnected stories that build on and refer to each other. These stories have been written and told for nearly a thousand years, dating back as far as fifth-century Welsh myth. Much medieval literature, from romances to epics, is built on the stories of the king of Britain, his knights of the Round Table, and the ultimate downfall of his court. This part of *The Books of Magic* utilizes some of the more obscure stories from the medieval Arthurian legend.

As Tim and Rose follow the path, they approach a hill ringed with standing stones and guarded by a giant. Doctor Occult (who has changed back to male) wins a riddle game against the giant so they may enter a cave in the hill, where a young man with a harp is singing about kings asleep underground. The minstrel turns out to be Thomas the Rhymer. Thomas of Erceldoune is a historical figure from the late twelfth century; the story found in the romance ("Thomas of Ersseldoune") and ballads ("Thomas the Rhymer") were attached to him later. During his life, however, he seems to have been renowned as a prophet.[9] Next to Thomas is a sleeping king—Arthur, he says. Or maybe it is Brian Boru (Ireland, c. 941–1014 CE), or Knez Lazar (Serbia, c. 1329–89 CE), or Charlemagne (Carolingian Empire, 748–814 CE), or any of the kings who are said to be asleep, not dead, waiting for their people's time of greatest need. This conflation of heroic nation-building kings mirrors Gaiman's later conflation of archetypes in the court at the end of the universe.

The link between Thomas the Rhymer and Arthur is thin but not nonexistent. The structure of the fourteenth-century romance has three parts: Thomas's trip to Faerie and his return, a selection of prophecies he received from the queen of Faerie, and a selection of more traditional prophecies discussing events dating back to Arthur and the Saxon invasion. Also among the stories added to Thomas's legend is an incident in which Thomas shows a horse trader a host of sleeping knights, which Sir Walter Scott links to Arthur. Robert Southey has suggested that Thomas's under-hill abode is the same one where Arthur and his knights are sleeping, waiting for the hour of greatest need.[10] Gaiman's placement of Thomas in Arthur's resting place under the Eidolon Hills, then conflating Arthur with the other kings Thomas mentions, is part of a medievalist tradition wherein (semi)historical figures are protagonists of fantastic stories, their mythologies often combined.

Thomas calls the giant outside the barrow Maugys. Of the Arthurian references in this passage, Maugys is perhaps the most obscure. He seems to come from an Old French Arthurian romance, *Li Biaus Descouneüs,* which was translated and adapted into Middle English as *Lybeaus Desconus* in the fourteenth century. It's a fairly standard "fair unknown" story; in this one, a young man sets out to prove his knightly prowess and turns out to be the bastard son of Sir Gawain. In *Li Biaus Descouneüs,* Malgiers li Gris is the suitor and guardian of the maiden la Pucele; in *Lybeaus Desconus,* he is transformed into Maugys, a giant who serves as champion for an evil sorceress.[11] Lybeaus, after a long and messy battle, defeats Maugys in single combat.[12] For Tim and Doctor Occult, getting past Maugys is much easier; he threatens to chop them into tiny bits, but Doctor Occult manages to talk him into a riddle game instead, which Doctor Occult wins almost by accident. Fortunately, Gaiman and Charles Vess, who did the art for this issue, chose not to follow the description of Maugys from *Lybeaus Desconus,* which relies heavily on medieval English demonization and stereotypes of Muslims and Middle Easterners. Giants are often used in medieval romance to denote outsiderness, violence, excess, and evil. While Gaiman's Maugys does threaten violence, he is nonviolently defeated and does not appear again.

The conversation with Thomas the Rhymer and all the threads of

Arthurian romance and Scottish folktales that go with it get more complicated when a brief mention of a link between Hell and Faerie is added; they "have always been linked—by right of tithe, if nothing else," Rose tells him.[13] This is the only mention of this tithe in *The Books of Magic*, but it's a much larger plot point in the concurrently running *Season of Mists*.[14] The stories of Thomas the Rhymer—a medieval romance and a later ballad based on the romance—are one of the places this tithe, or tiend, is mentioned in folklore. The other is "Tam Lin." Every seven years, the devil comes to collect his fee: a selection of people to take back to Hell with him. Tam Lin begs his lover, Janet, to rescue him because "I am so handsome and healthy / I'm afraid it will be me."[15] The queen of Faerie sends Thomas away at the end of seven years (or three, depending on the version) for the same reason:

> In the morning, the foul fiend
> Will take his fee from among these folk
> And you are so large and handsome
> I'm certain he'd choose you.[16]

There's no single, clear reason why Faerie would owe this debt to Hell; as best as anyone can tell, they are considered to be soulless, or fallen angels who didn't quite become demons, or a species that predates humanity and thus does not fall under God's pacts with humanity.[17] Faerie is its own separate realm in both the DC Comics/Sandman universe and in the Thomas the Rhymer ballads. The queen of Faerie shows Thomas three roads: one to Heaven, one to Hell, and one to Faerie. This places Faerie at a similar metaphysical level with Christian afterlives.

Faerie isn't the only place Gaiman invokes. Tim encounters a figure out of Arthurian legend: Merlin at age fourteen. Despite his youth, Merlin knows what's going to happen—that his grand experiment of Camelot is doomed to failure and he will be imprisoned in a cave.[18] However, echoing Morpheus in *Season of Mists*, he says, "I must do as I will do," and warns Tim that magic always has a price.[19] Like most

Arthurian characters, Merlin has been written and rewritten for thousands of years, including in the DC Comics milieu, where he has been a recurring character in various franchise lines since 1936. In addition to the adjustments necessary to fit his story and character into DC Comics' overarching mythology—including *The Books of Magic*—their version of Merlin seems to be based most heavily on Sir Thomas Malory's *Le Morte d'Arthur*. Interestingly, as Merlin relates his future to Tim, he seems to believe that Camelot could have lasted forever if it wasn't for his own weakness for Nimue. Those familiar with Arthurian legend will be aware that the reasons for the fall of Camelot are complicated, and it's unlikely that Merlin could have stopped it even if he had been there. But human weakness and ill-advised romances are foundational to the story of Arthur and the fall of Camelot, so it makes sense that Merlin would believe his own will contribute to it.

Merlin's appearance here is an exemplification of the history the Phantom Stranger has been showing Tim—a heavily magical, mythologized one. Tim sees the fall of Lucifer and of Atlantis, then travels quickly through probably ten thousand years of human history before he asks for a break. Merlin is the only medieval figure Tim sees; the Phantom Stranger takes him straight from ancient Greece to pre-Arthurian Britain, then to what looks like an early modern witch trial. Thematically, Merlin makes sense; every magical figure Tim encounters tells him that magic isn't worth it, that he shouldn't get involved. An ancient sage in the last days of Atlantis calls it "a big golden crock"; at the other end of history, at the court at the end of the universe, the Fool (who looks remarkably like Constantine) tells him that magic is dangerous.[20] As a cautionary tale about magic not living up to its promise, Merlin is a strong choice for an exemplar.

....

MEDIEVAL TAROT APOCALYPSE

At the end of the universe and all time, only archetypes are left. In an architectural scrap heap of a planet/city, Tim encounters the last remaining creatures in existence: the court of the Terminus. Everything has collapsed to its fundamental parts, and all the souls in history are contained in a few bodies. In order to represent these bodies, Gaiman chooses the Major Arcana from tarot, and they are represented with art that evokes a high medieval court. Yet the art is expressionist—a contrast to the realism of earlier issues and even earlier pages within this issue. Nothing here is solid. Panels differ in shape and size, often overlapping; sometimes the characters appear to be melting.

Tim and Mister E are greeted by the Hierophant, an old man in regalia that echoes the Catholic pope, but instead of crosses, his pallium is decorated with goblets or cups, one of the suits of the Minor Arcana. He explains to Tim that he is "all the hierophants there ever were, all the popes and priests and shamans and wizards, *all* of them."[21] He escorts them to the throne room, where the Empress and Emperor sit in an otherwise empty court. The only other figure we see is the Fool; the Emperor and Empress remark that the Lovers are gone, as are the Magician and the Hanged Man.

The history and origins of tarot are fuzzy, but it seems to have developed from playing cards in the late medieval and early Renaissance periods. It wasn't until the late eighteenth century that tarot decks were used for cartomancy and divination. Helen Farley argues that the rise of Romanticism and its fascination with the occult was a reaction against the heavily scientific, rationalist Enlightenment, which in turn was an attempt to separate society from what they saw as medieval superstition.[22] Romanticism tended to be medievalist, a nostalgic desire to return to a (nonexistent) past when life was simpler and people lived in harmony with nature.[23] In the late 1800s, the European interest in world religions and magical systems culminated in the founding of the Hermetic Order of the Golden Dawn, the most famous member of which was Aleister Crowley. *Sandman* readers will recognize the Golden Dawn's tendency to mash together various belief systems—Farley lists "Egyptian mythology, kabbalah, tarot, Enochian magic,

The Hierophant represents all priests of all religions across all time; his stole emphasizes the tarot inspiration for the Court at the End of the Universe (*The Books of Magic*).

alchemy, Rosicrucianism and astrology"[24]—from Gaiman's Order of the Ancient Mysteries, which captured and imprisoned Morpheus.

The Golden Dawn take on tarot has remained influential on modern usage and beliefs, which brings us back to Gaiman's use of tarot figures as archetypes at the end of time. Rachel Pollack, who advised Gaiman on tarot,[25] describes the sequence of the Major Arcana as a story of an innocent—the Fool—who encounters various figures as he travels.[26] This isn't unlike Tim's own journey; he has traveled all of time and space by this point. It is notable, then, that the tarot figures appear in reverse order—first the Hierophant (numbered V), then the Emperor (IV), the Empress (III), and the Fool (0). Tim is counting down to the end of time, not setting out on a new journey.

Interestingly, when Tim thinks he sees John Constantine, he isn't personifying the long-missing Magician but rather the Fool. Tim asks him for a lesson in magic anyway, and he responds (while performing sleight of hand) that he doesn't know anything about magic except that it's dangerous. He is accompanied by a butterfly, a warning that small changes can lead to catastrophic results. Earlier in Tim's journey, Doctor Occult describes Constantine as a man who "dances on the edge of the known," and Constantine is the only one of the Trenchcoat Brigade who doesn't claim to have all the answers regarding a right-and-wrong, science-versus-magic view of the universe.[27] An admission of lack of knowledge aligns Constantine with the Fool, but the Fool also represents a willingness to learn—a trait that Constantine and Tim share.

The Books of Magic showcases Gaiman's particular interests when it comes to medievalist mythology in a more compressed form than the much longer *Sandman*. He once again utilizes existing mythologies, especially those attributed to the Middle Ages, as well as the dream vision form, which gained in popularity and was refined as a literary device in the Middle Ages. He also uses the symbolic and metaphorical structures and language of fantasy literature to explore a particular worldview, also common for medievalist fantasy. In this case, the worldview is that modern life doesn't preclude magical thinking, that wonder is still possible in the modern world and doesn't need to be regulated to the past, and that fantasy and reality are both valid, are both necessary, and both serve a purpose in a healthy worldview.

CHAPTER FIVE

"To the World"

Good Omens and the Apocalypse

In the 1990s, as is traditional around the turn of a millennium, people began thinking and worrying about the end of the world. There was an uptick in doomsday cults such as the Branch Davidians, Heaven's Gate, and Aum. Films were full of catastrophes, from world-ending meteor strikes to runaway artificial intelligence to alien invasions. Tim LaHaye and Jerry Jenkins started their sixteen-book series on the Christian apocalypse. Software engineers went to work to head off the Y2K bug to prevent a serious problem when the calendar turned over from '99 to '00.

Of course, Neil Gaiman and Terry Pratchett teamed up to poke fun at the whole thing.

Good Omens: The Nice and Accurate Prophecies of Agnes Nutter, Witch, is a comedic novel set vaguely in the early 1990s, originally conceived as a riff on Richmal Crompton's Just William series (1922–70) with the Antichrist as the William figure. However, as Gaiman notes, "it rapidly outgrew that conceit and became about a number of other things instead."[1] Perhaps the most recognizable antecedent is *The Omen* (1976), a film in which an American diplomat in Rome unwittingly adopts the Antichrist; several plot points (the hellhound, the Antichrist as the son of Satan, a Satanic nanny) are clearly represented in *Good Omens*—not to mention the obvious parallel in the title. But *Good Omens* also, in true Gaiman and Pratchett style, pulls on dozens of other influences and traditions, from Christian apocalyptic millenarian dispensationalism to new age worries about science and the environment to the witch trials of the 1600s.

With an eye specifically to medievalism and medieval(ist) influences, *Good Omens* relies heavily on the idea of the apocalypse as described in the biblical book of Revelation and its interpretation throughout the Middle Ages. It also contains a nod to the medieval genre of saints' lives and hagiography—one that, despite its brevity, shows a knowledge of the tropes of the genre and plays with them. Finally, in the 2019 Amazon Prime TV series based on the book, we get a traditionally anachronistic look at Arthurian England.

Broadly speaking, *Good Omens* is a novel about religion and how people approach it, whether taking it too seriously or not seriously at all. Gaiman and Pratchett use the Christian apocalypse as a framework for exploring human responsibilities to each other and the planet, arguing that constantly expecting and waiting for the end of the world is ultimately detrimental to both. For frequent readers of both Gaiman and Pratchett, their individual styles are clearly visible—Pratchett's silly irreverence that barely disguises serious social and political issues, Gaiman's tendency to layer millennia of storytelling and traditions into a modern framework. The authors create a seriously funny—if at times dated, at least for a twenty-first-century audience—call for people to, as the angel Aziraphale describes Christ's message, "be kind to one another."[2]

REVELATION AND THE APOCALYPSE

The idea of the end of humanity is not unique to the Middle Ages or even Christianity. Ancient religions have had End Times mythologies since the beginning of religion, mostly based on seasonal cycles of death and rebirth.[3] Zoroastrianism has Frashokereti, Judaism has the end of days, and Norse mythology has Ragnarök. For the most part, Christian eschatology has trickled down from Zoroastrianism through Judaism, but over the centuries, other beliefs and approaches have been layered over even the biblical accounts that the idea is based on—mostly Daniel, Ezekiel, 2 Thessalonians, and Revelation—leading to millenarianism and the idea of the Rapture. The most prominent aspects of Revelation—the four horsemen, the Antichrist, signs and wonders, the plain of Megiddo—are present in *Good Omens*, giving the novel the framework of Christian eschatology even as it raises questions about the wisdom of relying on prophecy or waiting for the end of the world.

Christian theology of the Middle Ages weighs heavily on modern Christian theology and thus on some of the core concepts in *Good Omens*. Armageddon or the apocalypse as we conceive of it now would be alien to John of Patmos, who wrote the prophecies that became Revelation around 70–90 CE. The word "apocalypse" didn't originally mean "the end of the world"; per the *Oxford English Dictionary*, it comes from the Greek *apokalypsis*, which means "to reveal" or "unhide"—basically, "revelation." It wasn't used to mean an extreme disaster until about the 1850s. Taken as a historical work, the purpose of John's Apocalypse was to reassure and console the audience while warning early Christians, particularly those of the churches named in the early chapters, against being seduced by Roman ways of life.[4] The assumption was that Christ would be returning soon, but when he failed to appear, interpretations of Revelation and the other biblical books used as prophecies for the apocalypse shifted to the spiritual. Late classical thinkers such as St. Augustine (354–430 CE) pushed for a nonliteral interpretation, arguing that the war was within the Church and the human heart, and that the Antichrist was an internal evil, not necessarily an external one.[5]

Others, however, insisted on a literal end-of-the-world reading, focusing especially on the millennium. This focus comes both from Zoroastrianism—in a cyclical view of history, a thousand years is "a humanly conceivable time-frame"[6]—and Revelation's reference to the thousand-year reign of Christ. A belief in a literal End Times naturally leads to the question of when it's going to happen, the calculation of which involves a great deal of numerology, mapping the symbolism of prophecies onto contemporary people and events, and a belief in both divine ordination and human free will.[7] This type of belief also allows people to see meaning in disasters; for example, one of the most famous extant sermons from medieval England comes from a priest named Wulfstan (d. 1023 CE). His "Sermo Lupi ad Anglos" (Sermon of the Wolf to the English) is a fire-and-brimstone condemnation of the English, blaming the ongoing Viking raids on their own sinfulness and warning of the oncoming end of the world:

> Beloved men, know what the truth is: this world is in haste, and it approaches the end, and therefore it is ever worse and worse within the world. And so it shall necessarily become very much worse because of the peoples' sins before the arrival of the Antichrist, and then it will be especially dreadful and terrible throughout the world.[8]

Each generation that believes itself on the cusp of the end of the world sees its particular issues in light of symbols from the various apocalyptic prophecies.

In addition to religious doctrine about the impending end of the world, Gaiman and Pratchett also lean on the apocalyptic genre—that is, a popular culture structure of storytelling about the end of modern society (at best) or the entire planet (at worst). While ancient and religious apocalypses have clear motifs, when the idea moves into secular popular culture, those motifs may or may not carry over, instead shifting to purely secular threats such as zombies.[9] *Good Omens* also includes the threat of climate change, alien invasions, and nuclear disasters.

Gaiman and Pratchett approach the topic of the end of the world comedically and satirically in order to make a point about the particular mind-set of apocalypticism in general and millenarianism in particular. Most of the novel points out the uselessness of prophecies, even when they're correct; titular witch Agnes Nutter's prophecies are "nice and accurate," but they are useless until after the fact. As Agnes's descendant, Anathema, explains, "Most of the time she comes up with such an oblique reference that you can't work it out until it's gone past, and then it all slots into place."[10] Unlike the other prophets mentioned in the novel—Nostradamus, Mother Shipton, John of Patmos—Agnes's prophecies are focused entirely on her own descendants, who just happen to be involved with the end of the world, and thus are mostly useless for larger global applications. Anathema points to a few instances where small, highly specific prophecies were thought to have larger implications, mirroring the ways in which people try to map the prophecies from Revelation onto the modern world.

Attempts to decode Revelation or other apocalyptic texts are fundamentally about trying to understand a divine plan, and *Good Omens'* core argument is about the futility of these attempts. From the very beginning of the novel, in the Garden of Eden, the demon Crawly/Crowley questions his and his angelic counterpart Aziraphale's understanding of their own roles and choices. He has just finished tempting Eve to eat the fruit, and Aziraphale gave Adam and Eve his flaming sword as they were on their way out. "Funny if we both got it wrong, eh?" he tells Aziraphale. "Funny if I did the good thing and you did the bad one, eh?"[11] Without knowing God's ultimate plan, they can't be sure whether they're following it or not. A bit later, the narrative voice lays this thesis out in even stronger terms:

> God moves in extremely mysterious, not to say, circuitous ways. God does not play dice with the universe; He plays an ineffable game of His own devising, which might be compared, from the perspective of any of the other players,* to being involved in an obscure and complex version of poker in a pitch-dark room, with blank cards, for infinite stakes, with a Dealer who won't tell you the rules, and who *smiles all the time.*
>
> *i.e., everybody[12]

At the end, Metatron and Beelzebub are made to stand down by Crowley and Aziraphale asking if the Great Plan they keep talking about is also the Ineffable Plan—that is, the one that nobody knows but God. As Pratchett scholar Daniel Scott notes, the end of the novel shows that any Divine Plan is "so far beyond the reckoning or relevance of humans as to be moot."[13] Even the angels don't know the hour, as the Gospel of Mark points out (Mark 13:32). Thus, attempting to decode God's plan is not only a waste of time but actively detrimental.

Another point of pushback in the novel is against one of the fundamental beliefs involved in apocalypticism: that the end of the world is inevitable and desirable because it will lead to the ultimate punishment of the wicked and reward the righteous. This idea is presented in the novel through Adam, who declares that the world is so messed up that it's better just to start over, to "save the ones we want and start again."[14] Scott notes that this line of thought is "not merely reminiscent of eschatological concepts like Noah's Ark or Judgment Day—it encapsulates the thought process that essentially gave rise to them."[15] By putting these ideas in the mouth of a child, the authors argue that the ideas themselves are childish or childlike—an oversimplified way of looking at the world.

However, Adam pulls himself back, realizing that his ideas and world-ending impulses are harmful to himself as well as the world because he actually has the power to pull them off. While his core complaints—that adults are polluting and starting wars and otherwise making the planet a more hostile place to live—are legitimate, he realizes that ending the world isn't the answer. Instead, he argues with Metatron that "if you stopped tellin' people it's all sorted out after they're dead, they might try sorting it all out while they're still alive."[16] People's focus, the authors argue, shouldn't be on the end of the world but on continuing to make a better world to live in now. They don't just implicate religions in this argument either; by introducing Adam to Anathema's environmentalist, more new age approach, they also implicate secular defeatism. The future, they argue, is not fixed; it can be changed if people are willing to do the work and change it.

By the end of the novel, it seems that the idea of any sort of big plan and the prophecies that provide humans hints about it have been rejected, proven false by the premise of the book. However, the door is left open for another apocalypse down the road. Whether this was to leave room for a sequel or to walk back some of the rejection of prophecy isn't entirely clear. But it does seem that a new apocalypse is coming, and that Adam may play a role in it. This possibility is built through several details. Crowley and Aziraphale discuss the quiet as Heaven and Hell have stood down, and Crowley thinks the real "big one" is still coming—"all of Us against all of Them."[17] He argues that Adam's refusal couldn't have happened unless God wanted it to, that there are bigger plans than Creation and Apocalypse in the works.

The TV adaptation abandons a lot of the millenarianist thinking because Gaiman updated it for its 2019 release. Instead it leans harder on the themes of free will and ineffability, mostly by increasing the direct conflict between Crowley and Hell, Aziraphale and Heaven, and Adam and Satan. All three reject their assigned roles in the apocalypse, and Crowley and Aziraphale abandon Heaven and Hell for earth—and each other. The idea of a Divine Plan is much more central, with the archangel Gabriel visiting Aziraphale frequently to discuss the coming war. When Aziraphale tries to convince him that they can stop the whole thing from happening at all, Gabriel says, "Of course there [has to be a war]. Otherwise how would we win it?"[18] Like many apocalyptic thinkers, both Heaven and Hell (represented by Gabriel and Beelzebub) see earth and all the people who would die in the nuclear war as necessary collateral damage. But Crowley, Aziraphale, and Adam all recognize that the earth is quite nice actually, and worth saving as it is rather than destroying it to start over "just to see whose gang's better," as Adam puts it.[19]

Overall, Gaiman and Pratchett start from a foundation of highly recognizable, mostly Christian apocalyptic symbols, such as the Antichrist and the Four Horsemen, and bring humor to bear on them to portray them and most apocalypse ideas as fundamentally flawed to the point of absurdity. Scott calls this "secularization and de-mystification," arguing that the authors use the traditions of fantasy to "implicitly question Revelation's validity and applicability to our real world."[20] The metaphysics of prophecy and supernatural beings are shown to be less powerful than human action; Crowley complains to himself that "nothing he could think up was half as bad as the stuff they thought up themselves," like the Spanish Inquisition, [21] echoing Lucifer's complaint in *Sandman* that people keep blaming him for their own bad decisions. At the same time, the humans in the story are mostly narrow-minded or narrow visioned; even those who believe in the supernatural and recognize that the apocalypse is coming only see it through their own narrow viewpoints, such as Shadwell's insistence on only reacting to witches and not any other type of threat, or Anathema following Agnes's prophecies in lockstep.[22] As the authors explain early on, stating another thesis of the book, "It may help to understand human affairs to be clear that most of the great triumphs and tragedies of history are caused, not by people being fundamentally good or fundamentally bad, but by people being fundamentally people."[23] And while people have help from Aziraphale and Crowley, it is people who stop the apocalypse—at least for now.

....

MEDIEVAL WOMEN'S HAGIOGRAPHY

One of the ways Gaiman and Pratchett create humor in *Good Omens* the novel is through inversion; they flip what we would normally expect from a person or situation upside-down. In a lengthy gag early on in the novel, we're introduced to an order of Satanic nuns, the Chattering Order of St. Beryl. The immediate humor comes from several inversions. The nuns are Satanists rather than Catholic, they take vows to talk incessantly about whatever's on their minds rather than of silence, and when they can't speak openly, hijinks ensue (such as mixing up babies, one of whom is the Antichrist). Tucked in a footnote is the history of the Chattering Order of St. Beryl, which continues the humor through inversion while hitting nearly every trope seen in medieval hagiographies, especially those of women. Stories of the lives, deaths, and miracles (both before and after death) of saints were a popular genre in the Middle Ages, with hundreds of collections circulating throughout England, Europe, and the Near East during the era. The saints in question ranged from late antiquity through the contemporary age of the writer; often it behooved a small church to have a local saint as a tourist draw.[24] The story of St. Beryl Articulata of Cracow is dated to the "middle of the fifth century" in the novel, placing it in the tradition of early Christian martyrs.[25]

In brief, St. Beryl was a Christian woman married off to a "pagan." She prayed for intercession and was given the "miraculous ability" to talk nonstop. She was, the footnote tells us, either strangled to death three weeks after the wedding or lived to the ripe old age of sixty-two, her husband having procured a pair of earplugs.

Unwanted marriages, especially to pagans, are a staple of women saints' lives. These women either wish to devote themselves to God or specifically don't want to marry a non-Christian but are forced into marriage anyway. The stories of St. Agnes and St. Cecilia, both dating from late antiquity but spreading widely during the Middle Ages, involve Christian women married against their will to non-Christian Roman men.[26] Both women refer to Christ as their true betrothed or lover, refusing the attentions of their suitors and declaring their intentions to remain virgins. Cecilia fares rather better than Agnes: she manages to convince her new husband to convert to Christianity and allow her to remain a virgin. Agnes, in contrast, is forced into a brothel, miraculously saved from being burned at the stake, and then killed with a sword. Gaiman and Pratchett split the difference with two possible endings to St. Beryl's story. Either she is murdered in her bed (and still a virgin), or her husband learns to deal with her "blessing" and she lives happily into old age.

In most hagiographies, the women in question are saved, if only temporarily, from their fate by miraculous intervention. However, what is truly saved is not their lives—most of them are martyred—but their "virtue." Some convince their husbands to allow them to live as virgins, sometimes taking holy orders and leaving the marriage, as in the case of saints Cecilia and Æthelthryth. Cecilia's husband is visited by an angel who confirms the truth of Christianity to him, and he converts; Æthelthryth's "purity" is protected by God in more mysterious ways through two marriages. Others manage to preserve their chastity but not their lives, like saints Agnes and Agatha. Agnes is dragged to the brothel naked, but her hair grows to cover her body, preserving her modesty; Agatha has a breast cut off and miraculously restored. Less is known about St. Wilgefortis, but her marriage-avoiding miracle included growing a beard, after which she was crucified.[27]

Some form of gender-bending was not uncommon in saints' lives; after all, the ultimate expression of devotion to God was complete virginity, which was thought to render the woman genderless.[28] Medievalist Leslie Donovan counts over eighty transgender or gender-nonconforming saints in medieval hagiographies, including St. Eugenia, who dresses as a man to get a better education and winds up abbot of a monastery, and St. Euphrosyne, who dresses as a man to escape an unwanted marriage and lives as a hermit in a monastery. Beryl, however, has no such inclinations; she is aware of the possibility of growing a beard, but she has no intention of keeping it once the marriage has been called off.

In another comedic inversion, instead of a miracle of gender nonconformity, Beryl's miracle is decidedly feminine: she's gifted with the ability to talk nonstop, "without pause for breath or food."[29] The saints' lives frequently include the women in question standing up to men in authority and boldly declaring their faith and intentions, displaying a mastery of rhetoric that was stereotypically unfeminine. Beryl's gift is also of speech, but in a stereotypically feminine way, leaning on the misogynist idea that women's speech is inconsequential, constant prattle. In many cases, the saints' speech is what leads to their deaths, as their refusal to submit to male authority drives the men into a rage. Beryl's does essentially the same, leading to her husband strangling her two weeks after the wedding.[30]

One of the ways that saints are venerated is by naming churches or holy orders after them; sometimes their stories were enshrined in liturgies and nuns' vows as they joined the orders. The comedic inversion for St. Beryl's order is that instead of taking vows of silence or virginity, her nuns take vows to speak their minds constantly—except on Tuesday afternoons, "when they are permitted to shut up."[31] And of course they are satanic nuns—not that they are particularly evil. The authors are quite clear that these nuns are mostly hereditary satanists, "brought up to it" and practicing out of habit rather than conviction.[32]

As brief and footnotey as St. Beryl's story is, it shows a familiarity with medieval saints' lives, particularly women saints' lives, and the common genre tropes of them. This familiarity is then used as a satirical commentary on everything from said saints' lives to monastic orders to modern religion. Because the majority of the novel satirizes Christian apocalypticism, which in modern times tends to be a Protestant preoccupation, this allows the authors to branch out and make fun of Catholicism and lapsed Catholics as well. After all, St. Beryl doesn't seem to have been a very good saint; she was more interested in avoiding marriage than wanting to remain pure and religious, and her martyrdom (if indeed it happened) was due to her nonstop talking, not her faith. Like their view on apocalypticism, the story of St. Beryl also cautions against using ancient stories as a model for one's current life.

MYTHOLOGICAL MEDIEVAL BRITAIN

In writing the scripts for the *Good Omens* TV series, Gaiman discovered that "if you break [. . .] the novel down into six roughly equal parts, you will be surprised to discover an almost complete lack of Crowley and Aziraphale in part three."[33] Because Crowley and Aziraphale were the central figures of the show, Gaiman fixed this issue by creating a long cold open for episode 3 that charts the history of their relationship over six thousand years. The chronological spacing is uneven, with three biblical scenes (the Garden of Eden, Noah's ark, Christ's crucifixion), one in ancient Rome, one in the Middle Ages, and then five in the modern era (Shakespeare, the French Revolution, Victorian England, World War II, and the 1960s).[34] The scenes overall show the trajectory of their relationship, from being outright enemies to reluctant allies to friends.

The Middle Ages scene is specifically labeled "The Kingdom of Wessex, 537 AD." Historically, 537 CE saw the Saxons settling in, having migrated in after Rome withdrew, pushing the British tribes north and west.[35] Saxon conversion to Christianity was underway but not yet complete, and the first Viking incursions were still about two hundred years away.[36] But rather than setting the scene among Angle, Saxon, and Jutish tribes squabbling among themselves for land, Gaiman chose the mythological history of Britain, specifically Arthurian Britain, and, as is traditional for Arthurian mythology, it is fundamentally anachronistic.

The existence of a historical Arthur is a matter of debate. However, the legend that grew up around him is entirely fictitious, built up over a thousand years of storytelling and co-opted for the political and social agendas of various writers, kings, and even American presidents.[37] The earliest lengthy treatment of Arthur's reign comes from Geoffrey of Monmouth's *History of the Kings of Britain* (c. 1136), a pseudo history that was intended to extend classical history (specifically Troy and the Romans) to the British Isles, partly to increase the importance of the British, partly to create a historical continuity where there wasn't yet one, and partly to establish the right of the Norman kings to rule over the isles.[38] The story of Arthur thus began as fictional and anachronistic, and it kept that tradition through the French courtly love stories of Chrétien de Troyes; the poems of Wace, Wolfram von Eschenbach, and Robert de Boron; Layamon, who translated the legend into English; and Sir Thomas Malory, whose *Le Morte d'Arthur* is considered the definitive Arthurian work. Each of these authors added ideas, characters, motifs, and plot points, layering in anachronisms as they went, not least of which is the presence of knights and a full chivalric system in what is ostensibly sixth-century Britain. Arthur is one of the core touchstones of medievalism, frequently unmoored in time, used to represent the entirety of the Middle Ages in a single word.

The scene runs a bit over two minutes and contains about as many anachronisms as you could want. The castle in the establishing shot is actually a water tower that, with all the fog and a careful camera angle, resembles a castle turret.[39] Aziraphale's armor is a mix of fourteenth-century helmet, fifteenth-century Italian breastplate, and sixteenth-century spaulders. Crowley's leans more Germanic but is equally late in dating.[40] Aziraphale's horse is wearing barding, a practice that didn't develop in Europe until the late Middle Ages;[41] the particular style the horse is wearing appears to be early sixteenth-century Italian. In fact, the costuming more closely resembles something from John Boorman's film *Excalibur* (1981) than anything a Saxon or Brythonic warrior would wear.[42] However, as with so many medievalisms, the idea isn't to accurately represent a specific period of the Middle Ages, title card date and location notwithstanding. Rather, the point is to evoke the medieval for the audience. The armor, the castle, the fog—all combine in visual shorthand to this purpose. The invocation

Aziraphale in early medieval Britain. His armor is a blend of late medieval French, Italian, and German elements (*Good Omens* episode 3). Courtesy of Amazon Content Services LLC and BBC Studios.

of Arthur and the idea of a golden age of Britain—Crowley complains that Arthur is spreading too much peace and harmony—also serve this purpose.

The placement of the scene is particularly interesting from a medievalism viewpoint; it follows three biblical scenes (mythological) and one Roman scene (classical). Popular imagination often sees the Middle Ages as a period of magic and high chivalry; classical Rome, in contrast, is viewed as a time of early science, philosophy, and rationality. Renaissance thinkers in particular saw the Middle Ages as a fall from grace, a sliding back into superstition that they were recovering from by returning to the ideals of the classical era.[43] In this scene, set in an incredibly early Middle Ages, we see a hopeful and peaceful time, Arthur ascendant with a literal angel at his side. However, for those who know the origins of the Arthurian legend, the date itself warns that it won't last; 537 CE is the date of the Battle of Camlann as recorded in the Welsh *Annales Cambriae*—the battle in which Arthur and Medraut clash and kill each other.[44]

Essentially what this scene does is attempt to encapsulate the entirety of the Middle Ages, especially the British/English Middle Ages, by using a nearly universally recognizable medieval story to represent it. The setting and costuming, like Arthurian legend itself, is built on hundreds of years of popular culture reimaginings of Arthur and the Middle Ages, all of which are read as medieval by a casual viewer. It invokes a broad medievality rather than focusing on a single historical incident. It also establishes that the world according to *Good Omens* contains more than one mythology, even if it is most heavily based on Christian apocalyptic mythology. After all, Arthurian mythology was integrated into Christian mythology with the introduction of the Holy Grail, so it isn't remarkably out of place for the story.

CHAPTER SIX

Poisoned Apples and Magic Roses

Fable and Fairy Tale

Fairy tales are a major vector of medievalism in modern culture, which is fascinating simply because fairy tales aren't inherently medieval. We've had stories like them—folktales, wonder tales, beast tales, and so on—since the dawn of humankind. Lots of work and theorizing has been done attempting to trace the origins of these tales back to ancient Greece and even Indo-European cultures, but as J. R. R. Tolkien (among others) has pointed out, the search for an ur-story is fruitless and pointless.[1] Even fully defining what we mean by fairy tale is futile, though people have tried. It tends to be an exercise in exclusion rather than definition—of deciding what is not a fairy story rather than clearly defining what is. I like literary theorist Brian Attebery's "fuzzy set" method of classification: genres do not have hard boundaries; instead, stories are grouped together to compare their similarities and cultural functions.[2]

Certain motifs and trends may carry through as stories are passed down, but stories fit the culture that tells them, and the meanings and interpretations of them change accordingly. As Gaiman puts it, "Of course, fairy tales are transmissible. You can catch them or be infected by them. They are the currency we share with those who walked the world before ever we were here."[3] Author and literary critic Marina Warner has cataloged several of these motifs and trends—things like intergenerational strife between women, predatory and abusive husbands or would-be husbands, cannibalism (often as a metaphor for high mortality rates), and incest. She also traces how these themes, motifs, and tropes have come up through biblical stories into medieval romances and hagiographies—and also into fairy tales.[4]

However, as technology has advanced, certain stories and their cultural ideologies have been cemented through print or film, and these tend toward the medievalist. Charles Perrault's books of fairy tales, for example, were some of the first illustrated editions, and the illustrations included crenellated towers, Gothic arches, and other markers of medievalism, even when those don't make sense for the story.[5] This medievalism continued through the Grimms' versions of the stories, who set their versions in a generic Middle Ages on the basis of their view that fairy tales started out as religious stories or myths, then lost their religious connotations and became fairy tales sometime in the Middle Ages.[6] Perrault and the Grimms used the Middle Ages as "a time of romance, adventure, and chivalry for children,"[7] partly because old stories carry weight and authority, partly because the Romantics idealized the Middle Ages anyway, and partly because the Middle Ages had come to be seen as the childhood of mankind.[8]

Now, of course, we have the Disney versions, which are many people's first introduction to these stories, and sometimes to the Middle Ages. In many cases the Disney version is seen as the authoritative, even original, version of the fairy tale in question.[9] As Warner puts it, "The disequilibrium between good and evil in these films has influenced contemporary perception of fairy tale, as a form where sinister and gruesome forces are magnified and prevail throughout—until the very last moment, where, *ex machina*, right and goodness overcome them."[10] In medievalist Paul Sturtevant's study of how understanding of the Middle Ages develops, he found that the idea of what and when the Middle Ages are is heavily influenced in childhood by popular culture, especially fairy tales, and especially Disney's fairy tales.[11] Even stories not technically set in the Middle Ages, like *Beauty and the Beast*, which takes place in the mid-1700s, carry medievalist motifs and icons such as castles, stained glass, and a courtly, chivalric romance plot. All of this is frequently contrasted with a progressive sensibility; Belle and her father are portrayed as more philosophically advanced than their peers,[12] *Sleeping Beauty*'s Prince Charming tells his father that he's living in the past by insisting on an arranged marriage—"This is the fourteenth century!"—and Princess Jasmine fights tradition to marry the man she loves despite his lowly birth.[13] Yet ultimately the stories still reinforce heteronormativity and traditionalist gender roles, enshrining them with the ideas of fate, true love, and magic.

But the stories don't belong to Disney; plenty of writers have retold, recast, and reworked these traditional stories with new themes, in light of new social mores and norms, and sometimes just to play and make something new. Sándor Klapcsik traces postmodern, rewritten fairy tales back to the early eighteenth century, almost immediately after Perrault and Madame d'Aulnoy released their fairy-tale collections. More recently, writers such as Robert Coover, Tanith Lee, Angela Carter, and Robin McKinley have taken on various fairy tales, retelling and reworking them.

Such retellings have multiple purposes and effects. Literary critic Jade Lum argues that fairy-tale retellings in particular are good for untraining certain mind-sets such as "hegemonic and heteronormative gender roles."[14] Warner also points out that retellings are useful for pushing back against corporatized storytelling like Disney's versions of the fairy tales:

> As individual women's voices have become absorbed into the corporate body of male-dominated decision-makers, the misogyny present in many fairy stories—the wicked stepmothers, bad fairies, ogresses, spoiled princesses, ugly sisters and so forth—has lost its connections to the particular web of tensions in which women were enmeshed and come to look dangerously like the way things are.[15]

Retellings, particularly those by individual authors rather than a corporate entertainment body like Disney, allow societal issues to be tackled by updating them to reflect new issues and the new ways they might manifest. "These stories have power," Gaiman once said to a group of academics who seemed detached from stories, beyond seeing them as curiosities of the past to be dissected.[16] Updating and adapting these stories helps them keep that power.

Yet frequently the setting of the stories continues to be medievalist —not always (Gaiman also wrote stories such as "Diamonds and Pearls," an updated and urbanized version of Perrault's "Diamonds and Toads"), but often enough that it deserves note. A preindustrial world, commonly understood to be medieval, is where we've put magic and princesses and happily-ever-afters for hundreds of years. There's an understanding that such things can't happen in a modern setting, that the innocence or naivety associated with fairy stories are by definition medieval. Fairy tales in particular have acquired the sense of childishness despite their origins as very much not children's stories, in a way that links them to this sense that the Middle Ages were also childish.

....

GAIMAN'S FAIRY-TALE RETELLINGS

Gaiman sees fairy tales and myths, like all stories, as mulch for the compost heap, noting, "Our imaginings (if they are ours) should be based in our own lives and experiences, all our memories. But all of our memories include the tales we were told as children, all the myths, all the fairy tales, all the stories."[17] He also notes that fairy tales have been defanged, retold, revived, and parodied (much like the Middle Ages), but when they're done well, they still have power.[18] Stories survive in the form our culture needs them to survive in, he argues, and though Disney may have a near monopoly on how we tell fairy tales, bits from the older versions still survive, even as other bits—the bits the culture doesn't need anymore—are abandoned.[19]

It's no wonder, then, that Gaiman's take on fairy tales—and many of his other stories, for that matter—often draws attention to the act of storytelling and how stories are passed down. This is obvious in *Sandman*, which is a story about telling stories, but it also appears in his fairy-tale retellings; the short story "Snow, Glass, Apples," for example, uses an unreliable narrator to shift the perspective on the story of Snow White, while *The Sleeper and the Spindle* allows (a different version of) Snow White to consider major motifs in stories like hers such as happy endings, a true love's kiss, and free will. Of readers, Leslie Drury says Gaiman is "utiliz[ing] their familiarity and associations with social repetition in order to explore human experience, emotion, and sexuality through the act of tale telling."[20] Gaiman uses the deep familiarity Western audiences have with stories such as "Snow White" and "Sleeping Beauty" to build new stories on, usually without overtly identifying which story he's retelling.

Gaiman doesn't just retell, though; he disrupts. His fairy tales may draw on familiar motifs and schemas, but they also "disrupt standard patterns" in order to "confront readers with the validity of the behaviors, systems, and assumptions that fulfil the metanarrative and its underpinning ideologies."[21] In other words, he presents the usual cultural expectations or tropes that we find in fairy tales and writes his stories in such a way that we question those expectations and tropes and the stories that support them. Sometimes he does this by literalizing the figurative, sometimes by taking the tropes or themes to their extremes, and sometimes by reversing the tropes entirely. He pushes us, the audience, into discomfort in order to get us to think about stories we may take for granted after having been exposed to them for most of our lives.

"SNOW, GLASS, APPLES"

Gaiman's "Snow, Glass, Apples" is a traditional fairy tale, but it has a twist that takes it into true horror. The story retells "Snow White," but the titular princess, rather than being the heroine of the story, is a vampire. "Snow, Glass, Apples" follows the "Snow White" story from the perspective of Snow White's stepmother, usually referred to as an evil queen. The unnamed queen marries the king and is quite happy with their marriage, though she senses something is wrong with the young princess, especially when the princess bites the queen on the hand and licks up the blood. After the king's death, the queen has her huntsman take the princess into the woods and remove her heart, which the queen hangs from her rafters. Following the traditional beats of the "Snow White" story, the princess is not actually dead, and the queen's attempts to kill her lead only to her own inevitable death at the hands of the princess and her prince. What Gaiman does change is the meaning of all these events, using them to question how we know what we know about the stories behind fairy tales—and all stories, for that matter. "Lies and half-truths fall like snow," the queen says, "covering the things that I remember, the things I saw. A landscape, unrecognizable after a snowfall; that is what she has made of my life."[22] The story we know, the version of "Snow White" familiar to modern audiences, is a lie, she claims, "a little truth to add savor to the dish, but mixed with many lies."[23] The true story, or the one the queen wants us to believe is true, dies with her as she is roasted alive in a kiln on the princess's wedding day. Gaiman literalizes the figurative language of the "skin as white as snow, lips as red as blood, hair as dark as ebony" descriptions of Snow White, asking what kind of creature has pure white skin and bloodred lips? He also asks what kind of person would fall in love with a presumably dead girl and insist on carrying her off?

Like most traditional fairy tales, Gaiman includes a medievalist setting. The world of the story is preindustrial and feudal; it feels medieval. The country is a small kingdom ruled first by a king, then by the narrator queen; she lives in a castle and dries herbs and fruits by hanging them from her rafters; and there's a spring fair every year. Ideas often attributed to the Middle Ages also show through. For example, the queen mentions at least twice that the king was exercising his rights when he had sex with her, then carried her off to marry her. While not directly called such, this idea echoes *prima nocta,* an apocryphal idea that a feudal lord had the right to have sex with a bride on the night of her wedding before her husband.

The story also carries undertones of the idea that the land and kingdom mirror its ruler; feminist theorist Elizabeth Law argues that the king, with his red-bronze beard and "skin tanned the gentle brown of ripe wheat," embodies autumn, and the princess embodies winter.[24] Under the king's rulership, the land thrives; when the princess deposes the queen, all indications point to forthcoming cold, starvation, and death. The queen can be aligned with spring; she is associated with the spring fair, productivity, and renewal. She also cares for the people and is said to rule wisely—until the princess and her prince twist the story and recast her as the evil witch stepmother who tried to murder the innocent princess. The princess cannot overthrow the queen alone; it requires the help of her prince, who is sexually attracted to death, and the people themselves, who turn on her because, Law argues, "it is easier to believe in a cannibalistic evil stepmother than it is to believe in a strong woman, ruling fairly and independently of a man."[25]

Despite its overtones of pure horror, "Snow, Glass, Apples" is not without its traditional fairy-tale romanticism. While it doesn't rise to the level of Disney romanticism (there are no delicate, multispired palaces or happily-ever-afters here), the queen follows a familiar trajectory in her early story. We learn that she began as something resembling a peasant, telling fortunes at the spring fair and helping people find lost children and livestock by scrying in reflective surfaces. She dreamed of the king long before she met him, and she cast a glamour on herself and purposefully waited for him to cross her path in order to catch his attention. Then she married him and became queen. It's a rags-to-riches story aided by magic; Law compares her story to Cinderella if she acted as her own fairy godmother.[26] Unlike many fairy-tale heroines, who are often the beneficiaries of pure coincidence or the actions of others (like the prince or the fairy godmother), the queen takes her fate into her own hands.

Gaiman also readultifies the story. Like many fairy tales, "Snow White" has been toned down quite a bit from the "original" Grimm version for the more familiar-to-modern-audiences Disney version. The Grimm version included attempted cannibalism, attempted child murder, and torture. The Disney version skipped the queen eating what she thought were Snow White's internal organs, aged the princess up enough that it wasn't really child murder, and had the queen struck by lightning rather than dance to death in hot iron shoes. Gaiman's version includes vampirism, overt and at times transgressive sexuality, necrophilia, and torture. This is not a story meant for children, just as they weren't when the Grimms originally compiled them.

Besides the content, the thematic depth and breadth also removes "Snow, Glass, Apples" from the realm of children's stories. Gaiman isn't just creating a twisted, gory version of "Snow White" but questioning cultural assumptions like female beauty standards, expectations of patriarchal cultures, and even why fairy tales are told the way they are. This is accomplished through almost complete inversion of the core horrors of the story. Instead of a queen who practices child murder and cannibalism, the horror of "Snow, Glass, Apples" is centered on a vampiric young girl and her necrophiliac prince. Gaiman also inverts the usual fairy-tale ideas of naturalness versus unnaturalness; Law points out that the stepmother is usually the villain because of her intrusion into the family unit and her unnatural place in it, while the princess is usually shown to be at harmony with nature through her interactions with animals and time spent happily in the forest. Instead, the queen is aligned with nature, fertility, and spring, while the princess is a "thing."[27] This inversion extends to the fairy-tale trope of intergenerational strife between women by making the younger of the two, not the older, the dangerous aggressor.[28]

The sex at the core of the story is an important and persistent part of how the characters interact with each other. It's also another way that Gaiman inverts traditions and cultural expectations. Most readers are probably familiar with the virgin/whore dichotomy, a trend in literature examined extensively by critics such as Simone de Beauvoir and Laura Mulvey, in which women are considered either completely chaste and innocent or wanton and promiscuous. In the fairy tales, the princess (or the girl who will become a princess) embodies innocence, moral purity, and often passivity; the female antagonist (the evil queen/stepmother) embodies excess, arrogance, and independence. In "Snow, Glass, Apples," Gaiman flips this, but not by making the queen chaste—rather, by allowing her to have a healthy sex life and linking the princess's vampirism to sex. When the king dies, the queen finds bite-mark scars all over his body, including his genitals. Gaiman allows the vampiric and incestuous implications of these scars to speak for themselves. The queen sees the princess in the forest pretending to be a sex worker to get a monk out of his clothes and biting him instead. Black gunk flows from between her legs, exemplifying the horror cultural systems have for female sexuality, especially when uncontrolled by a man.

The princess simultaneously embodies and critiques the ideas of purity and the monstrous feminine by being an extreme example of both. As literary theorist Jane M. Ussher explains, one way women's bodies are idealized is through statuary, especially marble statuary: cold, white, and frozen.[29] Law points out that although Snow White is characterized by three traits—black hair, red lips, and white skin—her name centers whiteness and purity.[30] Portrayals of women like this strip away the messiness of humanity, especially the perceived messiness of postpubescent female bodily functions. Instead of making the princess the ideal of purity, Gaiman combines her with the monstrous feminine, both by making her a literal monster (a vampire) and by linking her with bodily fluids—not just the vampiric taking of blood, but the black fluid that stains her thighs. Menstruation is often treated as dirty, and women's bodies therefore as both polluted and threatening to men.[31] Gaiman literalizes this pollution and positions the princess as a threat to men and the male power structure.

But all of this is told in first person by a dying queen, and we are clearly meant to question her veracity. She's a witch, after all; she used magic to ensnare the king and to attempt to kill the princess while she lives with the dwarves. As literary critic Sándor Klapcsik points out, Gaiman's fairy-tale retellings tend to "replace the seemingly omniscient and reliable narrators with overtly unreliable narrators who are involved in the plot."[32] While fairy tales as we know them, be they those of the Grimms, Perrault, or others, usually have reliable narrators who stand outside the story, Gaiman gives us an entirely human narrator, one with her own agenda, biases, and viewpoint. Yet we, the readers, are her only audience. She refuses to explain to the people who are facilitating her death: "My soul and my story are my own, and will die with me."[33] She doesn't use her story to prevent her own death, only to further complicate a story that will be passed down as the truth. Drury argues that this shift in narration is meant to foreground how the story is told, not just the facts of the story; it brings the veracity of the entire story into question by upsetting the reader's belief in the previously known narrative.[34]

....

THE SLEEPER AND THE SPINDLE

For *The Sleeper and the Spindle*, Gaiman returns to a fairy-tale narrator, but in this case, he's telling a new story made up of familiar bits of old stories rather than recasting what we think we know about an old story. He returns to the Snow White story, but this time a Snow White years after the events of her usual fairy tale. She is not given that name, instead called only "the queen," leaving us to extrapolate which fairy-tale princess she is. On the cusp of her wedding, three dwarves come to tell her that a sleeping sickness is spreading through the neighboring kingdom. In order to protect her kingdom (and, not incidentally, put off her wedding), the queen crosses the border to save the princess, also never named but a clear Sleeping Beauty archetype. She works her way through the kingdom to the capital and up into the tower, where a beautiful woman is asleep in bed with an ancient crone watching over her. The queen kisses the sleeping woman awake, only to discover that she's the witch who cast the spell and the old woman is the princess; the witch's spell has leeched the princess's youth and beauty. After helping the princess kill the witch and rescue herself, the queen decides not to go home, but heads off to adventure with the dwarves.

The medievalism in this story is, like "Snow, Glass, Apples," immediately apparent from the setting, which is preindustrial and feudal. Magic abounds, from the spreading sleeping curse to the dwarves themselves, who aren't just humans with dwarfism but people who are magical by nature and have different bodily needs than humans (which protects them from the sleeping spell). The release of the story in an illustrated edition added more room for medievalism as well; the illustrations show interesting medievalist parallels. Each section includes a large first letter decorated with either vines or a stylized spindle, much like illuminated manuscripts did in the Middle Ages. And while the illustrations are mostly in black-and-white, most emphasize some facet of the picture with gold coloring, echoing the gold leaf used in illuminated manuscripts. Most frequently emphasized this way are the thorns on the rose vines, the interior pattern on the roses, and the dwarves' helmets, but illustrator Chris Riddell also uses it to draw attention to other thematic elements throughout the book.

Once again, Gaiman uses the familiarity of fairy tales to question or subvert the traditional cultural values found in these stories—in this case primarily patriarchal heteronormativity and passive female main characters. The queen is ruler of her kingdom in her own right, and Gaiman tells us very little about the prince she's about to marry. He's barely a blip in her overall story; he's mentioned as the queen prepares to leave, but even when the dwarfs discuss her previous magical sleep, they don't mention his (presumed) role in waking her. Gaiman and Riddell strongly imply that she was a warrior before she settled in to rule; she already owns weapons and armor, which Riddell shows discarded in a corner in a two-page illustration that centers the queen and her wedding dress. We're not told anything about her adventures, but it seems clear that she's had them.

Now, however, she's about to get married, which is the traditional ending of fairy tales. Rather than looking on her impending wedding with joy, the queen sees only how it will end everything:

> It would be the end of her life, she decided, if life was a time of choices. In a week from now, she would have no choices. She would reign over her people. She would have children. Perhaps she would die in childbirth, perhaps she would die as an old woman, or in battle. But the path to her death, heartbeat by heartbeat, would be inevitable.[35]

Riddell emphasizes the idea of endings with a golden skull pattern on the queen's bedclothes. Later, during her dress fitting, he accentuates the ribbon wrapped tightly around her waist, equating the dress and thus the wedding with restrictiveness; literary critic Danielle Russell equates the dress with a shroud.[36] The queen doesn't see her wedding as the culmination of her story, her happily-ever-after, but as a soft death before her true death.

It's no wonder, then, that when faced with the peril over the border, she decides to take care of it herself rather than sending someone. She leaves her kingdom in capable hands, notably not those of her prince, and goes on a quest to save a princess, thus taking on a traditionally

Chris Riddell emphasizes certain elements in his illustrations with gold leaf; the skulls on the queen's bedclothes represent her sense that marriage will be the end of her life (*The Sleeper and the Spindle*).

male role. As Anna Katrina Gutierrez puts it, "In claiming the quest/rescue motif for herself, she gains the agency typically reserved for Sleeping Beauty's prince, whereby she becomes integrated with schematic masculine performance and breaks away from the passive Snow White role."[37] This is also the first (but not the last) point in the story when the queen refuses to fit into a mold dictated to her by others, as

Lum has noted.[38] Rather than follow the trajectory of a fairy-tale heroine, whose story ends at marriage, the queen extends her story through changing her role.

Gaiman does not, however, make her into a woman acting like a man, as has been known to happen in fantasy texts featuring warrior women. Rather than being truly feminist, these texts merely insert women into a male power structure, either as an exceptional woman or, as Marleen Barr has it, as "sword-swinging men with female bodies and female names."[39] Gaiman's queen, though she carries a sword and wears armor, does not fight; she leaves the large creature Riddell places in the underground tunnels to sleep, and runs from the zombie-like sleepers controlled by the witch rather than cutting them down. "There is no honor," she insists, "in fighting an opponent who has no idea that you are even there. No honor in fighting someone who is dreaming of fishing or of gardens or of long-dead lovers."[40] She also doesn't fight the witch, mostly because that's not her fight. She hands the means to defeat the witch over to the princess and lets her do it for herself. This isn't to say that the queen is above violence. During a hallucination brought on by the sleep spell, we learn that the queen made her stepmother/witch dance to death in the iron shoes. It simply isn't her first impulse, the way it frequently is for male fantasy and fairy-tale heroes.

Yet the queen also doesn't quite fit into the standard fairy-tale heroines' ways of dealing with the problem, even the more active fairy-tale heroines. Warner points out that traditionally, women in these stories talk or magic themselves out of trouble.[41] This queen doesn't say much, and she doesn't do magic. What she does have is experience with this exact enchantment and this exact kind of witch, so she has a natural resistance to both. She spent a year in a glass coffin in an enchanted sleep, so she resists the sleeping spell. She's faced her stepmother, a witch who she says was more powerful than this one, and her memory of her stepmother helps her recognize the same threat of abuse and manipulation from the witch: "Learning how to be strong, to feel her own emotions and not another's, had been hard; but once you learned the trick of it, you did not forget."[42] The queen is a survivor of an abusive relationship. She can recognize another pattern of abuse and help the princess extricate herself from it.

The kiss is another way that Gaiman subverts traditions of fairy tales that usually reinforce heteronormativity and feminine passivity. It's established early that the kiss is the "usual method" of waking a princess in this circumstance.[43] No mention is made of true love being involved in this kiss, but neither was true love (or, often, a kiss) involved in breaking spells in the Grimms' fairy tales. Thus, when the queen arrives in the chamber where the witch is in her enchanted, parasitic sleep, she takes on the duty of kissing her "long and hard" to break the spell.[44] Lum reads it as utilitarian, entirely lacking in eroticism,[45] but the two-page illustration of the kiss imbues it with heavy romantic overtones and gives it far more weight than the text itself. Yet having the queen deliver the spell-breaking kiss inverts the usual gender roles and allows for a queer reading of the story, at least for a moment, until the sleeper's true identity is revealed.

The queen's choice to give the princess the means to free herself also subverts a number of fairy-tale tropes. It is another case of the queen's refusing anyone else's role in the story; she doesn't take responsibility for killing the witch, and thus she does not become the rescuer/prince figure. She leaves immediately after the evil is vanquished, taking no praise or reward. Traditionally the reward for this service would be the princess's hand in marriage, but the queen has already shown that she doesn't want to be married, and the princess (who has been awake for the duration of the curse) needs a nap more than anything. Gaiman also subverts the usual fairy-tale trope of women in conflict. The queen and the princess work together to defeat the witch, and the queen empowers the princess to do it herself, sharing her experience and knowledge to help the princess.[46]

Where this story still fits with standard fairy tales is in its ending—not in the facts of it but in the themes. Warner says fairy-tale endings are meant "to reveal possibilities, to map out a different way and a new perception of love, marriage, women's skills, thus advocating a means of escaping imposed limits and prescribed destiny."[47] In most fairy tales, this means the woman escapes peril in order to marry a prince, ensuring a life of safety and plenty. But over the hundreds of years we've been codifying fairy tales, that ending has become an imposed limit and prescribed destiny. Gaiman's queen moves past that, into a more modern happy ending, one in which she makes the choice *not* to get married, to have children, to rule her kingdom—at least, not yet. At the beginning of the story, the traditional path was a prison, a straight march to her death; at the end, she realizes that "there are always choices"[48] and forges her own path—forward into more adventure.

CHAPTER SEVEN

"Go and Catch a Falling Star"

Stardust and the Fairy-Tale Tradition

Of all of Neil Gaiman's fairy tales, *Stardust* is probably the most aware of its own heritage, perhaps because it was one of his earliest novel-length works.[1] Initially released as a four-part comic from Vertigo with illustrations by Charles Vess in 1997–98, *Stardust* was subsequently published as a novel in 1999, then adapted to film in 2007. Partly positioned as a reply and rebuttal to John Donne's "Song,"[2] which Gaiman uses as an epigraph, *Stardust* not only uses and fuses centuries of fantastic literature but also layers them in such a way that the layers are visible. As Gary K. Wolfe puts it, "Self-consciously derivative in both form and language, *Stardust* nevertheless may be counted among the more accomplished of contemporary fairy tales and represents an important step toward Gaiman's mature, distinctly literate voice."[3] *Stardust* contains clear allusions to medieval romance and Victorian fairy tales (which were deeply medievalist themselves), but it is a modern fantasy with modern sensibilities that invert or subvert traditional tropes and themes.

FOUNDATION OF MEDIEVAL ROMANCE

I've mentioned previously that modern fantasy shares a great deal with medieval romance, being very nearly directly descended from the genre. Medieval romance is a foundation of *Stardust*, as it is a foundation of most fantasy literature. Specifically, it provides the aesthetic and ethos of Faerie, which is set up in contrast to England in order for the main character, Tristran, to have his magical adventure. Like medieval romances, modern fantasy allows writers to explore societal issues at a remove, using metaphor and symbolism rather than looking at them directly. In the medieval romances, these issues tended to be, as medievalist Gail Ashton puts it, "dynastic inheritance and marriage, social ties and identities, and noble birth versus personal merit."[4] Medievalist W. R. J. Barron likewise points out how modern fantasy uses romance motifs:

> The court gathered around an archetypal feudal monarch in embodiment of chivalric values, the challenge to those values which its reputation provoked, the solitary quest of its representative along forest pathways to answer that challenge, the temptations which beset him in welcoming wayside castles, the lovely woman wooed and won among a maze of adventures, the eventual victory in combat against the challenger and eventual return to court.[5]

Romance and fantasy play on ideals, offering a world in which everything is eventually put to rights, characters reach their highest potential, and justice is done. In romance, this is focused in and around high royal courts, usually the court of Arthur, and the hero must travel out of that court in order to start his quest. The "other worlds," outside of court provide a contrast to the familiar world, "valorizing certain of its elements or aspects and offering visions of what it is not, and provide representations of its materially or morally unrealizable aspirations."[6] In *Stardust*, the familiar world is a mundane village rather than court, but the attitudes of the inhabitants of Wall are played as humorously pompous. Romance is also heavily symbolic and fantastic, with porous boundaries between the real and the supernatural, and multiple possible meanings for allegories and symbols.[7]

As literary critic Paula Brown notes, the names of the main characters in *Stardust* evoke medieval romance: the name of the main character, Tristran, echoes Tristram from the romances of Tristram and

Isolde, while the name of the star, Yvaine, echoes Yvain of Chrétien de Troyes's *Knight with the Lion*.[8] (Stars in Faerie appear as young women in silver gowns, but if they cross the Wall, they turn into earth's version of meteorites: dead rock.) These names cue readers to think of Tristran as a lover figure, specifically a medieval one, but without layers of association that something like Lancelot might include. It is interesting that Gaiman didn't choose something similar to Isolde for the star, which would have made the association much clearer. Instead, he chose Yvaine, the feminine version of Yvain, putting her in the position of knight errant herself rather than the knight's passive love interest.

While the plotlines of the Tristram stories[9] and *Knight with the Lion* don't line up with *Stardust* in any meaningful way, there are still trope and theme similarities with both these specific romances and romances in general. Tristran, for example, falls into the trope of "fair unknown," which I touched on briefly in chapter 4. Basically, fair unknown was a romance trope in which the hero has noble blood, is the son of a knight, or is in some other way better than the common folk, but he doesn't know it. He might leave his home in search of his fortune and a place in King Arthur's court, demonstrate prowess, and then be revealed to have been a member of the aristocracy all along. A medieval example of this is the French romance *Le Belle Inconnu*, a romance about a son of Gawain, but the motif also appears in Chrétien's *Story of the Grail*, among others. This is closely related to the trope of "blood will out"—nobility will become evident despite efforts to hide it. Medievalist Steven Knight classifies the fair unknown as a motif of a larger romantic structure, "knight-alone," in which "an unmarried hero [. . .] wins his way to a wealthy wife and so establishes both a family and his own honor."[10] These romances, like *Stardust*, center such problems as isolation, a lack of honor or status, and "the need to have female company in order to be both honored and wealthy."[11] Identity is deeply important in the romances, with the quests and such serving as a crucible for the protagonist to discover who he really is.[12] Tristran begins his quest in an attempt to woo Victoria, but in the process he falls in love with and eventually marries Yvaine; it is, as Gaiman's first line tells us, a story of "a young man who wished to gain his Heart's Desire," though that desire isn't initially what he thinks it is, and he himself isn't who he thinks he is.[13]

Like the knights Gingalain, Perceval, and Gareth of the various fair unknown romances, Tristran is unaware of his Faerie heritage, though in his case, it's flipped from the usual form of the romances—his mother is from Faerie and his father is a regular mortal man. Tristran decides to go to Faerie to fetch a fallen star, but his father, Dunstan, sees it as a sign of his blood calling him. Even when Dunstan explains to the guards on the wall why they should let Tristran through, Tristran doesn't fully understand. Only at the end of the book is he told first about his Faerie heritage, then about his birthright. Hints of both appear throughout the novel, but Tristran doesn't have a frame of reference or enough information to make the leap from inexplicably being able to navigate in Faerie to being the heir to Stormhold. Yet the truth of his heritage comes almost as an afterthought and is clearly not the most important thing about him. Gaiman glosses over Dunstan's conversation with Tristran explaining everything, and Tristran tells Una, his mother, that he doesn't particularly want to be lord of Stormhold. He also refuses to travel back to Stormhold in grand style with her, instead going on foot with only Yvaine, then going off to experience Faerie. Fair unknown romances do not extend to preternatural abilities in politics and war; instead, Tristran spends eight years learning about his kingdom and meeting his people before he takes charge.

Another medieval romance trope in *Stardust* is the fairy lover, probably most prominent in Marie de France's *Lanval*.[14] In this romance, a lesser knight of King Arthur's court, Lanval, is wooed by a fairy queen, who showers him with gifts and riches. She says she is all his—but only if he doesn't tell anyone about her. Lanval ultimately breaks this promise, but the fairy queen rescues him from a trial for treason and carries him back to Faerie. Wild Eadric, an early English magnate turned folktale, similarly runs across a group of ladies, one of whom becomes his fairy wife, and the legend that they rode through Wales persisted at least into the nineteenth century.[15] Melusine, the subject of several romances, is a fey creature said to be the mother of several European rulers and the founder of the fortress of Lusignan. Giving powerful figures and families supernatural or legendary origins was not at all unusual for medieval epics and romances.[16]

The fairy lover trope, when it involves a female fairy and a male human, is very much about sex and sexuality. The introduction of a fairy and of Faerie allows the narrative to explore certain features of sex and relationships that would have seemed problematic to a medieval audience.[17] In *Stardust*, the fairy lover trope marks the story as adult; the sex scene between Dunstan and Una is moderately explicit and takes place in the first chapter. It's also transgressive, an unplanned sexual encounter between a fairy and a human who's been courting someone else. There's no discussion or even suggestion that Dunstan should stay with Una, and he goes back to his normal life. In this case, it's a plot device to set up Tristran's birth and his heritage, which are central to the rest of the story.

Tristran is the one who carries the fairy lover plot through to its end; while Dunstan returns to England and raises his family, Tristran stays in Faerie with Yvaine. Like Lanval, he disappears into the other world, never to return. However, there's a slight twist to the fairy lover trope in Tristran's case; his relationship with Yvaine is much more chaste, almost asexual. On the page, they kiss once, and despite the length of their marriage, they never have children. This is not to say that Gaiman intended that Tristran and Yvaine never have sex, but it is an interesting inversion of a trope that is so heavily involved with sex and sexuality. Paula Brown argues that this creates a sense of a "pure" love between

Tristran and Yvaine, one that echoes a Petrarchan-era "sad passion" of a poet for a lady who is "impossibly remote, inconceivably perfect, who is, alas, ultimately unobtainable."[18]

Like most fantasy with clear ties to medieval romance, *Stardust* includes magic quests and allegorical encounters. In Tristran's quest to retrieve the star, he is hindered by the Lilim, who want the star to regain youth. The romances are full of fairies, witches, and fairy witches who hinder the protagonist; Morgan le Fay is the most famous of these, appearing in dozens of romances and usually complicating things for the protagonist, be it Arthur, Lancelot, Tristram, or Gawain. This also isn't the first time Gaiman has used the Lilim; the term appears in *Sandman* as well. In Jewish mythology, the *lilin/lilim* are demons, possibly descendants of Lilith, associated with the night and often portrayed as succubi.[19] Gaiman frequently literalizes nursery rhymes, giving them immense power in Faerie or showing them acted out; the magic candle is one example, as is the unicorn-versus-lion battle. While the nursery rhymes in question are allegorical, they also have literal impacts on Tristran's story. He travels via candlelight using a traditional nursery rhyme:

> How many miles to Babylon?
> Three score miles and ten.
> Can I get there by candlelight?
> Yes, and back again.
> If your heels are nimble and light,
> You may get there by candlelight.[20]

Tristran also sees a unicorn and a lion fighting, echoing another traditional nursery rhyme that metaphorically describes the fraught union between Scotland and England. The unicorn helps Yvaine after its fight with the lion.[21]

Magic and magical realms are frequently coded as medieval, partly because of the nineteenth-century anthropological argument from

Andrew Lang and others that "myth and legend were the survival structures of primitive belief, embedding agricultural seasons into the narrative tradition," followed by the Romantics and their idea of the medieval sublime.[22] However, quite a bit of the novel, and the version of England Gaiman creates for it, is overtly Victorian, creating a fascinating contrast between England and Faerie, natural and supernatural, reason and superstition.

....

VICTORIAN FAIRY TALES

The opening pages of *Stardust* situate Wall in the United Kingdom, "a whole night's drive" from London.[23] The mention of modern transportation and road paving indicates that Wall still stands, as it has for thousands of years, steadfast in its duty to keep Faerie and England separate. Gaiman then backs up to Victorian England—an early Victorian era, when Queen Victoria was young, Charles Dickens was writing *Oliver Twist*, John William Draper had photographed the moon for the first time, and Samuel Morse had invented the telegraph. The specific people and incidents Gaiman lists date the beginning of the story to around 1840 CE. Draper and Morse in particular are meant to evoke scientific progress, usually seen as antithetical to magic and fairy tales; Gaiman says that if you'd mentioned magic to either of them, they'd have "smiled at you disdainfully."[24] Yet as literary critic Meredith Collins points out, Draper, Morse, and Dickens "could all represent Victorian human magic as well, all being figures of both renown and wonder, able to perform acts that most people cannot meaningfully comprehend, either in their own time period or ours."[25] The specific choices made in describing the early Victorian era, with a Queen Victoria with "apples in her cheeks and a spring in her step,"[26] projects a time of hopefulness and the possibility of magic. There is also a darker undertone that Gaiman doesn't explore; Dickens's *Oliver Twist* draws attention to issues of child homelessness, labor, abuse, and exploitation, but itself is almost a romance, with Oliver being a long-lost heir and ultimately adopted by a gentleman.

Victorian England was a time of major reinterest in fairy tales after active suppression by the Calvinists; while Germany and France saw publication of Johann Musäus's *Volksmärchen der Deutschen* (Folktales of Germany, 1782–86) and Perrault's *Tales of Mother Goose* (1697), England didn't see the rise of the literary fairy tale until the end of the eighteenth century.[27] Folk belief did continue, although the associated mythology itself didn't develop much past 1640 CE.[28] For the Romantics, writing fairy tales was in itself a form of rebellion against the utilitarianism of the Enlightenment, and such tales were frequently used for social and political commentary, often to the detriment of the art itself. Later writers—Dickens, for example, but also Lewis Carroll and George MacDonald—pushed back against this didacticism.[29] By the end of the nineteenth century, fairy stories were frequently outright subversive, hiding that subversion in nonsense. As literary historian Jack Zipes puts it, "For many late Victorian authors, the writing of a fairy tale meant a process of creating an *other world*, from which vantage point they could survey conditions in the real world and compare them to their ideal projections."[30] This is one of the core purposes and uses of medievalism in general and medievalist fantasy in particular, and the Romantics and Victorians were instrumental in creating the genre as we know it.

The Victorian era was also a time of renewed anthropological interest in folklore, again as resistance against the Enlightenment. Folklorists saw themselves as rescuing material before the utilitarians could wipe it out. The focus was often on where fairy belief came from and why a culture would have these stories; most frequently, fairies were traced back to pagan gods, with their roles and powers reduced as their worship died out. As Thomas Keightley put it in 1826, "all these beings once formed parts of ancient and exploded systems of religion, and [. . .] it is chiefly in the traditions of the peasantry that their memorial has been preserved."[31] John Black in 1806 claimed that belief in the supernatural came from a lack of scientific understanding:

> In such cases, where the ideas are few, fancy is ever busy to fill up the void which the uniformity of external objects leaves in the mind. The imagination blends itself with the reality, the wonderful with the natural, the false with the true. The ideas acquire strength, and mingle in such a manner with external impressions as hardly to be distinguished from them. And as the laws of nature are yet unknown, the problem of probability is unlimited, and fancy grows familiar with chimeras which pass for truths.[32]

Like much medievalism, fairies and belief in them were heavily tinged with nostalgia, a sense of something (childhood, a simpler past, history) lost to time, or in some cases colonialism. The modernization of the world, especially during the industrial revolution, was blamed for the loss of fairies in England, and fairies themselves became associated with nostalgia, a loss of innocence, and "the erosion of tradition by the demands of the present and the pressure of the future."[33]

It is in this mix of nostalgia for premodern, magical times and forward-looking scientific progress that Gaiman sets the England side of Wall. On the one hand is Dunstan, a sensible young man whose idea of courtship talk is "the theory of crop-rotation, and the weather," and who sees himself, as a citizen of England and Wall, as superior to all the "furriners" who come to town for the fairy market.[34] Despite this solidness of temperament and lack of imagination, Dunstan is charmed by the fairy market in general and Una in particular, but then he goes back to Wall, marries his sweetheart, and raises his children.

Tristran, on the other hand, is full of grand romantic ideas in a way that blends nineteenth-century boys' adventure tales, such as Robert Louis Stevenson's *Treasure Island,* and high medievalist romance. Tristran dreams both of sailing off to new lands to colonize "the savages" and, when the wind is right, of fantastic adventures in forests with princesses in need of rescue, knights, and fairy creatures.[35] This blend and its contrast with the much more sensible ideals of the other residents of Wall is most evident in Tristran's lengthy conversation with Victoria regarding the fallen star. Made bold by a wind out of Faerie, Tristran asks Victoria if he can walk her home (yes), then if he can kiss her (no), then if she'll marry him. She demands to know why she'd do such a thing, and he waxes rhapsodic about all the places he'd go and things he'd bring back for her—India, Africa, America, the Arctic, Cathay, Australia. His language is elevated, passionate (Gaiman calls it "grandiloquent");[36] hers is down-to-earth and sensible. As Paula Brown puts it:

> Tristran's language is characterized throughout his interchange with Victoria as ritualistic and mythological. He speaks as The-Hero-of-the-Tale, a chivalrous knight who is addressing a queen of the realm. Victoria, on the other hand, repeatedly undercuts Tristran's lordly proclamations by replying to him in a matter-of-fact language of easy familiarity. The conversation putters out in the comical failure of both parties to communicate.[37]

Tristran, whose name echoes a romance hero, and Victoria, whose name plants her firmly in Victorian England, fundamentally cannot understand each other. Tristran is heir to a fairy kingdom, but Victoria repeatedly reduces him to his current job as a shop boy, the implication being that a shop boy isn't good enough for her. When he declares that he will go and bring back the falling star, her response is "go on, then," but she doesn't believe he can do it, or that he'll even try. When he sets off, she laughs at him.[38]

Despite Victoria's attitude, she is not set up as one of the villains of the piece. Rather, she serves as the representative of Victorian England, an England that barely believes in magic. In the case of Wall, this disbelief is in the face of living literally on the other side of a wall from Faerie, with people traveling through at least once every nine years to go to the market. She and Tristran reflect opposite Victorian sensibilities, personifying the dichotomy Gaiman sets up in the opening—science and magic, sense and sensibility. She is also the catalyst that serves to push Tristran out of his stuffy Victorian world and into his adventure. Victoria represents home; the romance hero must leave home and go into Faerie to find his true love.

Along with societal parallels, *Stardust* also shares a decidedly feminist ethos with some Victorian fairy tales. Zipes claims that English fairy tales, as opposed to the German ones, "placed great emphasis on the fusion of male and female qualities and equality between men and women."[39] Female writers such as Evelyn Sharp, Mary de Morgan, and Edith Nesbit wrote stories centering on girls who take charge of their own adventures. George MacDonald also wrote stories in which the male and female characters realize that they are mutually dependent, pushing back against gender essentialism and advocating for introspection and self-awareness for everyone.[40] Tristran initially single-mindedly barrels into Faerie, his head stuffed full of the colonialist ideas that are at the heart of his boys'-adventure-story declarations to Victoria. When he finds Yvaine, he uses a bit of magic chain to bind her to him, treating her as an object rather than a person. Yet as they travel, Tristran begins to see her more as a person. He releases her from the chain, which later earns him the help of a nymph turned tree. He tells Primus he's looking for her to make amends for offending her, and he rescues her from the witch-queen. This rescue creates an obligation, and as they travel together, they grow fond of each other, to the point where Tristran is deeply conflicted about his vow to bring the star to Victoria: "the star was not a thing to be passed from hand to hand, but a true person in all respects and no kind of a thing at all."[41] He develops compassion and self-awareness, both of which help him to understand that he has been an idiot. He thus releases Victoria from her obligation, returns to Faerie to spend his life with Yvaine, and only then discovers his birthright, which he delays for eight years.

....

MODERN FANTASY

Being a modern story, *Stardust* of course carries modern and postmodern ideologies and themes layered in with the medieval romance and Victorian fairy-tale aesthetics. Like *The Sleeper and the Spindle* and "Snow, Glass, Apples," in *Stardust*, Gaiman disrupts some of these themes, pushing back on female beauty standards, the privileging of youth, and colonialist ideologies. This disruption isn't always entirely successful, and the possibility for misinterpretation is there.

Stardust is positioned, at least partially, as a response to John Donne's "Song," first published in 1633, placing it squarely between the medieval and the Victorian. "Song" offers a sequence of impossible tasks, such as "catch[ing] a falling star," and presents them as equivalent to finding "a woman true, and faire."[42] Donne's narrator says to tell him if such a woman can be found—but on second thought, don't, because by the time he gets to her, she'll be false. The poem itself might be satirical or represent the narrator's personal disillusionment with his love, but taken in isolation, it's a cynical, even misogynistic, poem.[43] Gaiman has said he liked but disagreed with "Song," and both show in the themes of *Stardust*. Paula Brown argues that *Stardust* is idealistic and metafictional, "questioning the *perspective* from which the typical post-modern reader views the fantastic quest."[44] She points out that at a surface level, *Stardust* seems to agree with "Song," but ultimately it "seeks to redefine both the nature of desire and the identity of the true lover."[45] Victoria and Yvaine aren't rivals or even opposites; they are just love interests for different stages of Tristran's life.

Tristran ultimately falls in love with Yvaine and releases Victoria from any obligation to him, but first he has to go through a great deal of adventure with Yvaine. The star is the center of the plot; Tristran wants her as a trophy, the Lilim want her heart to return their lost youth and beauty to them, and the princes of Stormhold need the jewel she's carrying in order to become lord. The Lilim in general, with the unnamed witch-queen as their representative, seek to capture Yvaine and remove her heart in order to eat it and regain youth, beauty, and power, which are inextricably linked.[46] Their conversation with each other makes it clear that they have hunted stars, killed them, and eaten their hearts several times before. The Lilim fill a standard fairy-tale role I've already mentioned: the older woman threatened by the younger, a representation of intergenerational conflict. Author and scholar Susan Cahill also reads this as a critique of the beauty economy; the Lilim's evil isn't being old and ugly but rather is "the acquisition of beauty through artificial means" and deceitful performance of the male ideal.[47] This is not unusual for female characters coded as monstrous; as literary theorist Barbara Creed points out, one way that woman as monster is presented is "through her evocation of the natural, animal order and its terrifying associations with the passage all human beings must inevitably take from birth through life to death."[48] The monstrous feminine is outside the natural order yet hyperassociated with nature to a grotesque degree, crossing into the abject. Abjection is a poststructuralist idea primarily about breaking borders—between human/inhuman, natural/supernatural, good/evil, cleanliness/dirtiness, childhood/adulthood. Things that offend or disturb the established social order are abject, though they are also part of the human experience and must be dealt with.[49]

Yvaine saves herself from them, rather than Tristran doing it for her. In an unusual turn for a modern fantasy, there is no set-piece battle with the witch-queen but instead merely a conversation. The Lilim cannot have Yvaine's heart, she explains, because it belongs to Tristran. The witch-queen says it's a waste of a heart—"Your boy will break it, or waste it, or lose it. They all do."[50] The fairy-tale witch is not fed into her own oven, or made to dance to death in iron shoes, or stabbed by the prince. Instead, she voluntarily gives up her hunt for the heart of a star and is sent home to live with herself and her sisters for however long she has left. Failing to achieve her goal is considered punishment enough.

Stardust's approach to aging is a bit uneven and in places gender essentialist; Matthew Crofts and Janine Hatter note that while the Lilim are seeking youth and Yvaine will always be young and beautiful, the story is ultimately about Tristran's growing into a man. He has several mentors in this along the way, all male: the Hairy Little Man, Septimus, Captain Alberic, and of course his own father. Aging is shown to be positive for men, who must grow into their ability to wield power.[51] Unlike the Lilim, none of the men shows any interest in Yvaine for her heart and its youth-granting properties; they're only interested in the power that comes with the stone that knocked her out of the sky. Similarly, on the other side of the wall, Victoria marries Mr. Monday, whom she'd initially dismissed as old—a whole forty-five years old, which to a seventeen-year-old is decrepit. He does, however, have a steady income, a nice house, and a coach-and-four, as Victoria's friend Lucy points out. When Tristran returns, Victoria tells him she loves Mr. Monday, though Crofts and Hatter argue that she's taking her place in the beauty economy, trading her youth for security and wealth.[52]

Yet while Yvaine appears to be the ideal woman for a patriarchal society that prizes women only for their youth and beauty, Gaiman pulls a bit of a twist. All of the hypermasculine, fratricidal princes die, leaving the son of their sister as the only heir. Tristran doesn't immediately take the throne, which allows Una, who was never even considered to be in the line of succession, to rule—and rule well—for eight years.[53] After Tristran dies, Yvaine rules in perpetuity. Instead of being the tool by which the throne is held for the male heirs, Yvaine herself remains in power.

Finally, Gaiman tackles the particular colonialist bent that frequently appears in the antecedents for *Stardust*. Boys' adventure stories in particular tended toward a go-forth-and-conquer/civilize mentality, which is on display in Tristran's declarations to Victoria that he'll go to places that he clearly has only a passing familiarity with. Curry notes that he treats Faerie just like these other places—just another exotic location to be plundered for its resources and used to impress Victoria, as fantastic and inaccessible as India or America.[54] Indeed, when he first crosses the wall, he retains his Englishness for a bit, thinking of the natives of Faerie as other and treating Yvaine like an object to be taken back to England. He resists wearing fairy-style clothing when his is destroyed, seriously considering going around wearing just a blanket, "like a savage aboriginal from one of his schoolbooks."[55]

However, Gaiman allows Faerie to speak for itself, first through Yvaine, who is not shy about telling Tristran off; she's also given the only profanity in the entire book. "You're a clodpoll," she says, "and a ninny, a numbskull, a lackwit and a coxcomb!"[56] All of these are synonyms for foolish, though the last one can also mean a dandy, which lines up with Tristran's issues with clothes, particularly his lost bowler hat. She continues to rebuke him throughout the book, though toward the end, her name calling becomes more fond and less angry.

Faerie, specifically the wild nature part of it, also has a voice in the copper beech tree that helps Tristran after he's lost Yvaine. She explains that Pan himself charged her with helping Tristran and offers a different theory of ownership than the usual colonialist one: "You just have to know that it's yours and then be willing to let it go."[57] She provides a cautionary tale for Tristran by explaining how she became a tree: "A nymph. I was a wood-nymph. But I got pursued by a prince, not a nice prince, the other kind, and, well, you'd think a prince, even the wrong kind, would understand about boundaries, wouldn't you? [. . .] But he didn't, so I did a bit of invoking while I was running, and—*ba-boom!*—tree."[58] The underlying warning is that Tristran is in danger of being the wrong kind of prince by tying Yvaine up, but by letting her go, he saves himself from that fate. The tree tells him that if he hadn't let her go of his own free will, if she had escaped instead, she wouldn't have helped him, no matter what Pan told her. Because he did, though, the tree gives him a great deal of help in finding and rescuing Yvaine from the witch-queen.

Part of Tristran's character development is in leaving behind the Victorian-coded colonialist outlook and instead becoming a true resident of Faerie—so much so that by the time he leaves Wall for the last time, it's as alien to him as Faerie was at the beginning. This shift in attitude shows not only in realizing Yvaine isn't a thing to be given away but also in smaller ways—helping a little woman set up her stall without being asked, refusing Una's pomp and circumstance, and traveling Faerie to get to know it before taking the throne. Curry says this is a reversal of the usual colonialist structure; the heroes of those stories often face a sense of displacement when returning home, but they are eventually reintegrated into "civilization." Tristran's reintegration is into Faerie, which frequently rejects the label of "civilized."[59]

Like many of Gaiman's works, *Stardust* uses and acknowledges its predecessors and influences, but it also brings a modern progressive sensibility, gently pushing back against harmful tropes or traditions. *Stardust*, in particular, leaves the layers of historical literary influence visible while including critiques of literary artifacts like medieval romances, Victorian adventure stories, and fairy tale. Gaiman gives a voice to the traditionally voiceless and offers a different way of looking at literary tropes we may have come to take for granted.

FILM ADAPTATION

I don't plan to spend a lot of time on the *Stardust* film (2007), mostly because Gaiman wasn't as involved with it as he has been in more recent screen adaptations of his work. But the film, which is delightful in its own right, makes some notable changes to the story that in some ways reverse Gaiman's core ethos. Victoria is villainized, the film is far more violent than the book, and the ending goes for happily-ever-after instead of tragedy. That's not to say that the film is bad, or even a bad adaptation, only that it does different things than Gaiman's book.

Where Gaiman characterized Victoria as practical and sensible, at odds with Tristran's tendency to flights of fancy, the film makes her a spoiled snob. This version of Victoria (Sienna Miller) is every inch Donne's untrue woman; she takes advantage of Tristan's (Charlie Cox) attraction to her in several small ways while calling him a "shop-boy" derogatorily and courting Humphrey (Henry Cavill), the local dandy. She sends Tristan out after the star in earnest, liking the idea of "my very own star," and gives him a deadline for returning. If he misses it, she'll marry Humphrey. This version of Victoria emphasizes that Tristan's quest to bring back a star in exchange for her heart is an exercise in poor judgment; he is mistaking beauty for goodness. Her deadline also adds some urgency and stakes to the plot, giving it a reason for moving as quickly as it does. When he does return, his confrontation with her and Humphrey demonstrates how much he's grown over the course of the film. He recognizes that not only was his infatuation with her childish but that she treated him badly, and he gets to show off a bit of the swordplay he learned in Faerie to best Humphrey, who thrashed him at the beginning of the film.

The hint that the film will feature more violence than the book comes early on, when Una (Kate Magowan) tells Dunstan (Ben Barnes) that her servitude will last until Madame Semele is dead, instead of when a set of esoteric and seemingly impossible criteria are met. And indeed, near the end, the witch-queen Lamia (Michelle Pfeiffer)[60] blasts Semele's head off with magic, tangentially freeing Una. Where this increase in violence is most noticeable, however, is in the climax. Instead of a quiet conversation and the witch-queen returning home to her sisters, the film gives us a massive set-piece battle in which all three witches and Prince Septimus, presumed heir to Stormhold, die. Septimus kills Empusa, Lamia kills Septimus, Tristan kills Mormo, and Yvaine kills Lamia; it's quite a bloody ending. The shift makes sense.

Film is a visual medium that thrives on spectacle, and after the swashbuckling adventure of the rest of the film, a quieter ending might feel like a letdown. However, as Cahill points out, the battle unfortunately reintroduces some of the gender issues that Gaiman had purposefully written out: "That *Stardust* stages the final battle as one that takes place between evil queen and younger heroine serves to emphasize this unease surrounding the older, more powerful woman who must be replaced by youth, innocence, passivity, and domesticity."[61] Crofts and Hatter also note that the film ending reintroduces fairy-tale binaries between age and youth, evil and good.[62]

Finally, the ending also leans more traditional, with Tristan becoming immortal because he "possesses the heart of a star" and, when their children are grown, traveling by candlelight to the heavens with Yvaine to live happily ever after. Rather than overturning the patriarchal order with Yvaine ruling alone forever, the line of the lords of Stormhold continues—probably with less fratricide. This is also an understandable change. The film is fun and uplifting; appending the book's ending would be a rude and jarring shift in tone. The ending also nicely bookends the beginning, which introduced us to the idea of the stars watching us back. The opening came in from the heavens, and the ending returns there.

Gaiman has pointed out that what readers will tolerate and even enjoy in a novel does not necessarily translate to what moviegoers will tolerate in a film.[63] Changes are necessary, good, and appropriate when moving a story from one medium to another. However, these changes can shift core themes, resulting in a different message than that of the original text.

CHAPTER EIGHT

"Loki Has Done This"

Norse Mythology

Until now, the novels and stories I've discussed have been (or have had major elements that were) strongly medieval inspired, borrowing themes, tropes, and structures from Western medieval literature. However, that's not the only way that Gaiman interacts with the literature and culture of the Middle Ages. He also sometimes directly adapts characters or stories. Three major works explore Norse mythology: *American Gods* (2001), *Odd and the Frost Giants* (2008), and *Norse Mythology* (2017); in addition, there are multiple mentions and representations of Norse characters in *Sandman*. While *Norse Mythology* was the last to come out, it is foundational, providing not only the original (so to speak) stories but also insight into Gaiman's thought processes and views regarding Norse mythology and its place in a modern world.

Adapting mythology can be difficult for modern writers, mostly because, as critic Kathryn Hume notes, the gods have attributes, not personalities or an inner life.[1] They do not grow or change; rather, they fulfill certain roles in the stories, and those roles match their established attributes. For example, Odin is wise and thoughtful; Loki is mischievous and tricky, bordering on evil; and Thor likes to hit things with his hammer. In *Norse Mythology*, Gaiman leans into this rather than struggling with it or adjusting it for a long-form narrative. Motivation is present for some of the gods some of the time, but frequently, they simply act according to their natures, with a step-by-step march toward Ragnarök and their inevitable end.

OVERVIEW AND CRITICAL HISTORY

Most of what survives of Norse myth is found in two texts: the *Poetic Edda* and the *Prose Edda*. Both manuscripts are Icelandic, and both date to after Iceland converted to Christianity in 1000 CE. The *Prose Edda* was compiled and edited by Snorri Sturluson, an Icelandic politician and scholar living in the thirteenth century. The material in the *Poetic Edda* seems to predate Snorri, although the surviving manuscript, the Codex Regius, dates to about 1270 CE. In the 1600s, the material was attributed to Icelandic scholar Sæmund the Wise (1056–1133 CE). This is almost certainly incorrect, but the dating has led to the *Poetic Edda*'s being referred to as the Elder Edda. It is impossible to date the actual poems in the Codex Regius, even in relation to each other.[2] One other copy of the same material exists in a manuscript that includes a few other poems not found in the Codex Regius.[3]

Snorri's purpose was not to preserve or propagate Norse religion but to preserve traditional poetic forms and terminology as well as to instruct new poets on their use. One of these poetic devices, kenning, refers to poetic allusive descriptions, many of which refer to Norse myth—for example, referring to "gold" as "Sif's hair." In order to explain these kennings, Snorri provides the stories behind them, many of which he borrows from poems found in the *Poetic Edda*. He frequently quotes from these poems within his prose retellings. The *Prose Edda* is divided into four parts, with subdivisions within these parts: Snorri's prologue; the *Gylfaginning* (The fooling of Gylfi), in which a Swedish king is given a huge chunk of mythology during an extended vision; the *Skáldskaparmál* (The language of poetry), which provides stories explaining certain kennings and allusions found in Norse poetry; and the *Háttatal* (List of meters), which demonstrates differences in poetic meter and poetic devices.[4] For those interested in the stories, the *Gylfaginning* and the *Skáldskaparmál* are the most useful and interesting, and they are also where Gaiman gets most of his material for *Norse Mythology*.

While Snorri provides some context for his stories, the *Poetic Edda* collects mostly contextless poems. The first, the *Völuspá* (Seeress's prophecy), is an accounting of the creation of the world and some of its creatures, certain incidents in Asgard, and finally Ragnarök. The dense and scattershot verses are loaded with allusion, making it all too easy to miss what is actually happening, which is that Odin is consulting a seer about the end of the world. Odin's asking questions about Ragnarök or otherwise seeking wisdom is a common theme early in the *Poetic Edda*. Snorri's approach is far more readable for a modern audience, but the *Poetic Edda* has more material and stories; it is just more work to tease out the narratives.

In addition to making the stories more accessible, Snorri also argues for recognizing the importance of the Norse mythological cycle to be just as high as classical Greek and Roman myth; he attempts to "harmonize" Norse traditions with Christianity.[5] His prologue begins with Adam and Eve, explains how human expansion led to some cultures losing knowledge of God, and ultimately claims that Odin was a direct descendent of Priam of Troy. Euhemerizing—that is, writing histories in which gods were originally human and only came to be considered gods centuries later—pagan gods was not unusual for medieval Christian writers. Per Snorri, the Æsir were humans elevated to godlike status, and their descendants became rulers of much of Europe.[6] The prologue serves two purposes: first, to argue that although Iceland had previously been heathen, they were not "doomed souls in league with Satan" but rather lacked the information necessary to be good Christians;[7] and second, to argue for the historical importance and continuity of the Scandinavian kings. This sort of adjustment of history to bring northern Europe into the traditions of Greece and Rome in order to establish the legitimacy and importance of kings (or entire groups of people) was fairly common in the early Middle Ages; Geoffrey of Monmouth did the same thing for Britain in *History of the Kings of Britain* (c. 1136). According to Geoffrey, the British are descended from Brutus, son of Silvius, who is himself son of, yes, *that* Aeneas. Brutus rescued Trojans from slavery in Greece and fled to Albion, which they renamed Britain;[8] this lineage ultimately led to Arthur. Snorri wrote during the collapse of the Icelandic commonwealth, when Icelanders were eager to "see themselves as having achieved significant cultural and political achievements outside of the influence of Norway."[9] Other chronicles and collections of poetry were being written or compiled at this time as well, with an eye to preserving and elevating the history of Iceland.

What the Eddas don't provide is any idea of how the Norse religion was practiced. Snorri wasn't concerned with retrieving heathen rites or practices; as medieval linguistics scholar Tim Machan puts it, the *Prose Edda* is "fundamentally Christian in outlook. It remembers pagan gods and practices, but only through the lens of a Christian and following Christian exegetical traditions of compilation and synthesis."[10] Essentially what he did was take a set of loosely connected poems and myths, "often contradictory, incomplete, or obscure," and attempt to create a consistent, logical system out of them.[11] The disjointedness of the surviving material is more evident in the *Poetic Edda*, which is made up of dozens of poems and fragments of poems that deal with everything from the creation of the world to Ragnarök to various bits about the Nibelungs and the Volsungs.

Little surviving information exists about the religion behind the mythology, and what we do have mostly comes from outsiders such as Tacitus (*Germania*, late first century CE), Saxo Grammaticus (*Gesta Danorum*, c. 1200 CE), and Ahmad ibn Fadlan (tenth century CE). No clear or universal organizing principle seems to exist behind the religion; rather, it expresses "a common view of the universe and a belief in the same pantheon of Norse gods and other supernatural creatures."[12]

Sacrifice, human and animal, does seem to have been part of the traditional rituals, and annual ceremonies were observed in the usual times: fall, midwinter, and summer.[13] However, any surviving discussion or explanation of the religion comes from people who lived outside it, and none provides an exhaustive overview of how the northern pagan tribes worshiped.

Modern interest in and access to the Eddas only truly began in the late 1600s, when they began to be translated into English, primarily as a way to establish an origin story for the English people. Absent a similar mythology or study of poetics for Old English, scholars of early English glommed onto Snorri and generalized Icelandic Norse mythology and poetics across "Gothic" traditions.[14] Snorri's poetics were used to analyze and legitimize Old English poems such as *Beowulf*, and terms such as kenning and *heiti* (poetic simile) were also borrowed to discuss Old English poetry.[15]

For the most part, the Eddas remained obscure until 1770, when Thomas Percy translated chunks of them from a French edition into English in his *Northern Antiquities*. This is where the Romantic poets got their Gothic flavor—Valkyries, shield-maids, horned helms, drinking out of enemy skulls—mostly misinterpreted or mistranslated and leaning heavily on the perceived barbarism of the northerners.[16] A direct and full translation of the *Poetic Edda* arrived in 1866, when Benjamin Thorpe produced the *Sæmundar Edda*; by this point, however, interest had turned toward the sagas rather than the mythology. Early twentieth-century scholarship ignored the poems as art. Instead, attempts were made to mine them for historical information, "for reconstructing Indo-European mythological patterns, leading to an undue emphasis on seasonal and fertility motifs; for uncovering Germanic prehistory, giving life to forgotten heroes of the Migration Period (AD 400–600), and demonstrating Germanic ethics, customs, and heroic culture."[17] In the mid-twentieth century, attention returned to the poems as literature, with various literary theories being brought to bear on them.

Throughout these three hundred odd years, the myths and sagas influenced fiction writers, of course, notably J. R. R. Tolkien, who lifted many of the names of his dwarves directly from the *Poetic Edda*. Also on the list of twentieth- and twenty-first-century authors who have borrowed from or adapted Norse myth are Jack Kirby and Stan Lee (the Thor comics), Rick Riordan (*Magnus Chase*), Joanne Harris (*Runemarks, The Gospel of Loki*), Elizabeth Bear (*The Edda of Burdens*), Poul Anderson (*War of the Gods*), and even Michael Crichton (*Eaters of the Dead*).

Unfortunately, these myths have also been co-opted by white nationalist and white supremacist movements, most notably the Nazis. The Nazi party took nineteenth-century medievalism, such as the work of the Grimm brothers and Richard Wagner (composer of *Der Ring des Nibelungen*), and created a fictional Germanic ideal that was destined to rule over and eventually eradicate all other races—not that it took much appropriation to use these writers' work for this purpose; the Grimms had a nationalist agenda, and Wagner was straightforwardly antisemitic. The Nazis launched a campaign to research European and English folklore and myth to "invent a prehistoric pan-Germanic past, with or without the cooperation of the facts."[18] This myth of racial purity and white supremacist identification with Viking culture continued and continues; Norse myth, symbolism, and paganism are all clearly visible in twentieth- and twenty-first-century white supremacist movements and acts of violence.[19]

Thus, whether this was part of Gaiman's intent or not, a Jewish author retelling the Norse myths helps partly reclaim these myths from those who would use them for nefarious purposes. A book like *Norse Mythology* is an equalizer, offering the stories to everyone rather than hoarding them for only one specific race or ethnicity and thus helping these stories break away from connotations of white supremacy and violence.

....

GAIMAN ON NORSE MYTHOLOGY

Gaiman's specific affinity for Norse mythology began in childhood, first with Marvel Comics and then with *Myths of the Norsemen* by Roger Lancelyn Green; he says the stories felt true and right and familiar.[20] They resonated with him more than classical Greco-Roman mythology because Norse myth includes "flawed protagonists and a satisfyingly dark worldview."[21] His approach to writing *Norse Mythology* focuses more on the characters and story and less on the Eddic presentations of these myths. He describes the book as not a translation but rather a retelling of the Eddas that "loses a lot of those long goofy plots of the Eddas where Odin shows up in disguise and there are long questions and answers and people say: 'Well how *was* the world created?' and he says (in a very Odinic voice), 'I will tell you how the world was created.'"[22] He wanted to produce a book that wouldn't annoy a Norse scholar, but that wasn't written for a Norse scholar so much as to tell a good story.[23]

Initial reactions to announcements of the book were mixed, partly because the marketing implied that Gaiman was writing some kind of definitive Norse mythology. Some practicing pagans expressed concern that he would misunderstand or mangle their beliefs; others were excited that he'd be bringing their stories to a larger audience.[24] Reviewer Lisa Hannet says the "small-scale cultural appropriation debate" that sprung up in the comments to his Facebook announcement were due to the marketing "implication that Gaiman has altered, revised, remade, or somehow *improved* the source material."[25] Gaiman's approach to Norse mythology, however, is the same as his approach to any other text: they are stories, and stories survive in the form that their culture requires. They are not dead things to be encased in amber or, conversely, dissected; they are instead living reflections of culture.[26]

At the time he was writing *Norse Mythology*, the culture seemed to him to have clear reflections of Ragnarök. Between Brexit and the election of Donald Trump for president, Gaiman recalls feeling much like he did during the Cold War with its threat of nuclear war, but with a much more chaotic threat—"a million actions and inactions" instead of a single push of a button.[27] More than one critic—and indeed Gaiman himself—has noted the similarities between climate change and Fimbulwinter, the extreme, years-long winter that heralds the beginning of Ragnarök. Carolyne Larrington, a medieval scholar who has translated the *Poetic Edda,* has noted a resurgence in interest in Norse myth in the last twenty years or so, writing, "Our mounting fears that the folly of our rulers and the inevitability of planet-wide destruction will bring us all to catastrophe have become ever more culturally salient in the past few years."[28] As I have already noted, this is common for medievalism and medievalist texts. We find comfort in displacing our current problems onto the past, or remembering that people in the past had the same problems we do now—or at least the same worries and reaction to those worries.

Yet even Ragnarök isn't *the* end; it is simply *an* end, with a new world rising from the ashes of the old.

TEXT OF NORSE MYTHOLOGY

There's no sense in attempting to analyze *Norse Mythology* for accuracy to the original myths because no originals have survived, and the versions we do have are already "contradictory, incomplete, or obscure."[29] Snorri wrote down what was interesting or useful to him, and our extant versions are copies of copies of his originals, with all the problems that go along with that—missing pages, unreadable chunks, mistakes and interpolations and omissions by the scribes who did the copying. The same goes with the *Poetic Edda.* Whichever scribe compiled the volume saw particular worth in those poems, but the Codex Regius is also likely a copy of a copy. We have no idea what the stories would have sounded like to ancient or early medieval Scandinavian or Icelandic people, and if they had more stories or emphasized different parts of the stories, they are lost. Instead, as with any analysis of a medievalist text, it is far more interesting to look at how Gaiman adapted the material, what was interesting to him, and how he has adjusted it for a modern audience.

Gaiman's clearest priority is readability; also, he does not assume that the audience has any familiarity with the source material. Stylistically, his approach centers the action of the stories rather than the storytelling method, though hints of an oral tradition come through. The *Prose Edda* is presented mostly in dialogue, with someone (either Gylfi or Ægir) asking questions, while someone else (the Æsir or Bragi) answers the questioner, often in the form of stories. But these are not stories meant to entertain; they are stories meant to inform. As a result, they are frequently short and contain little in the way of character or dialogue. The poems in the *Poetic Edda* are likewise often expressed in dialogue, either actual or implied; in proverbs; or in fragments.

Gaiman modernizes the presentation of these stories, shifting nearly everything into third-person narration and adding dialogue and exposition that helps to make the stories more interesting to a contemporary reader. As reviewer Kimberlee Bartle notes, this also helps translate medieval Icelandic humor into something a contemporary reader would find funny.[30] However, he doesn't completely ignore the likelihood that many of these poems and stories were performed before they were written down. He uses periodic second-person narration to bring the reader into the experience—in fact, he begins the book with a second-person address, informing the reader, "Many gods and goddesses are named in Norse mythology. You will meet quite a few of them in these pages."[31] On two occasions, in the introductions to "The Mead of Poets" and "Ragnarök: The Final Destiny of the Gods," Gaiman instructs the reader to "listen" in order to learn. Bartle notes that not only does this "connect the story to an audial/oral experience," but it also echoes the *Völuspá,* in which the seeress frequently ends stanzas with, "Do you know yet, or what?"[32]

Another way that he helps to improve readability for a modern audience is through his method of collecting and synthesizing information. The things we know about the gods—specifically Odin, Thor, and Loki, whom Gaiman focuses on most strongly—are scattered throughout the Eddas and a bit into the sagas. Gaiman opens the book with "The Players," in which he provides descriptions of these three gods. These clear, compact descriptions, unlike the stories he tells later, are found nowhere in the Eddas. Yet for audiences who may be only vaguely aware of Norse myth, or even unaware of it entirely, understanding the stories' characters is important, so Gaiman provides a primer. This is especially helpful for Odin, whose character is complex and whose information is the most scattered among various original texts.[33] Snorri organized and condensed much of the information from the *Poetic Edda,* but even he doesn't fully introduce Odin until part 20 of the *Gylfaginning,* and this comprises a long list of names that Odin has gone by or that were given to him.[34] To readers unfamiliar with medieval Icelandic language and culture, the meanings and implications of these names are lost, so a list of names is of no help. Gaiman's approach is even simpler than Snorri's. He gives the reader enough to understand how important and powerful Odin is without overwhelming us with names. He does the same for Thor and Loki, although their characters are easier to parse out even in the Eddas.

This approach of collecting and synthesizing information from various places in the Eddas is a running theme for *Norse Mythology,* especially early on, when Gaiman discusses the creation of the world, the structure of the nine realms, and how Odin lost his eye and Mimir his head. After that, the stories are pretty much beat for beat the stories found in the *Prose Edda,* just rewritten for the sensibilities of a modern audience. However, scattered information isn't the only difficulty

Gaiman would have faced in these early sections; "The Players," "Before the Beginning and After," "Yggdrasil and the Nine Worlds," and "Mimir's Head and Odin's Eye" are pure lore, with a dearth of story or characterization. It's necessary information for understanding the cosmology of Norse belief and for fully appreciating the stories that follow, but it violates that most basic of fiction-writing rules: show, don't tell. To soften this, Gaiman relies on short sentences and simple words, with his style evoking a parent or a bard passing the stories on. Where possible, he adds narrative, turning a few lines of poetry into several pages of dialogue. For example, the source material for "Mimir's Head and Odin's Eye" is a few lines throughout the *Völuspá*, *Gylfaginning*, and *Ynglinga Saga*.[35] Gaiman chooses to relate the story primarily through dialogue. Odin approaches Mimir and asks for permission to drink from the well of wisdom, and Mimir refuses him—unless he sacrifices an eye. Odin agrees immediately. Gaiman establishes the core of Odin's character here. Odin is constantly seeking wisdom and is prepared to do whatever is necessary to get it. When the Vanir cut off Mimir's head and return it to Odin, his main concern is that Mimir's knowledge and wisdom are not lost, so he preserves the head, which will advise him as Ragnarök approaches.[36]

The path to Ragnarök is the central theme of the book; even in stories that have little to do with the climactic final battle, Gaiman works in hints and allusions to it. The stories he has chosen—only a fraction of those found in the Eddas—all have some part, however small, in explaining how and why Ragnarök happens. He states in the introduction that he sees the stories as "a journey, from the ice and the fire that the universe begins in to the ice and fire that end the world."[37] The stories that follow the lore setup of the first four sections are primarily from *Gylfaginning* and *Skáldskaparmál*, occasionally with details filled in from Snorri's sources in the *Poetic Edda*. To address the issue of the source material's sparseness, Gaiman adds detail, exposition, and a great deal of dialogue, most of which builds the conflict between

Loki and the other gods and establishes the resentment that leads to his role in Ragnarök. Other relationships and rivalries are also seeded throughout the text, most notably Thor and Jormungundr (aka the Midgard Serpent) and Odin and Fenrir.

Ragnarök is not so much foreshadowed as presented as a foregone conclusion. In "Before the Beginning and After," Gaiman lays out the shape of the world before Midgard was created, consisting only of Niflheim (darkness) and Muspell (fire). Surtr, who will burn the world at Ragnarök, has always already existed and is waiting in Muspell.[38] After Odin drinks from Mimir's well, he retrieves Mimir's drinking horn, called the Gjallerhorn,[39] and gives it to Heimdall so he can use it to warn the gods of Ragnarök.

Odin knows that Ragnarök is coming. While Gaiman skips Odin's visit to the seeress as depicted in the *Völuspá*, his drink from Mimir's well gives him foresight and wisdom. Yet he does nothing to attempt to stop it. Rather, the actions he takes or allows other gods to take could be seen as ensuring it comes about. He kidnaps and binds Loki's children, Jormungundr, Fenrir, and Hel, all but ensuring their enmity.[40] He allows Loki to be bound under the earth despite Angrboda's prophecy that Ragnarök will start when Loki breaks his bonds. While having the wall around Asgard built and gathering warriors at Valhalla to fight the battle of Ragnarök with him can be seen as preparation, they are clearly insufficient; Snorri has one of Gylfi's Æsir note that despite the sheer numbers of Einherjar in Valhalla, "even those will be thought too few when the Wolf comes."[41]

The central figure in Ragnarök, at least among the Æsir, is Loki. Loki's origins are fuzzy. He is the son of giants but is counted among the Æsir as Odin's blood brother. Gaiman says that even the gods "do not know when Loki came to Asgard, or how."[42] Loki helps the gods, but usually to get them out of situations he caused in the first place. Eventually he pushes them too far. Loki's sons are murdered and their intestines used to bind him under the earth, serpent's venom dripping into his eyes. This might be the last straw, but his resentment toward the gods is shown building over the course of the stories. Gaiman arranges the stories to show Loki's tricks escalating from rude but essentially harmless (cutting off Sif's hair) to exposing the gods to danger (helping a giant steal the apples of immortality), then finally to the outright murder of Balder, Odin's son and everyone's favorite god. Throughout these stories, the gods both threaten and execute physical violence against Loki. He is forced into undignified positions to help them and rarely acknowledged for his accomplishments, only his failures or tricks.

Gaiman does not shy away from the characterization of the other gods as generally unpleasant people; indeed, comparative religion scholar Kevin J. Wanner says part of Loki's role in the Eddas is to handle the gods' tendency toward "negative reciprocity," or a desire to keep the gods in charge and in possession of their things through any means necessary, even trickery.[43] Gaiman continues this characterization in *Norse Mythology*. This is clearest in "The Master Builder," in which the gods openly discuss among themselves how to get a wall, or most of a wall, out of the builder without having to pay him. Loki helps them devise the contract, then is charged with making sure the builder can't hold up his end. In order to do so, Loki transforms himself into a mare and entices the builder's horse away, becoming pregnant and giving birth to Sleipnir, the eight-legged horse that Odin rides. Gaiman portrays this as an embarrassment for Loki; he doesn't want to talk about it afterward, and he makes life unpleasant for anyone who brings it up. This is one of several examples in which Loki is humiliated to keep the status quo in Asgard. Is it any wonder, Gaiman seems to ask, that he turns on the gods at Ragnarök?

Ragnarök as we understand it is a traditional apocalypse scenario: the world becomes an inhospitable place; humans fight over resources and social systems break down; the sun, moon, and stars all disappear; and everything ends in a climactic battle that wipes out almost all the gods, the forces arrayed against the gods, and humankind. The individual fights on the plane of Vigrid, where the battle will take place, have been set up throughout the stories. Odin fights Fenrir, whom he betrayed and had bound. Thor fights Jormungundr, whom he's wrestled at least twice before. Frey, who once had a sword that could have defeated Surtr, dies for lack of that sword. Loki and Heimdall fight as they once fought over Freya's necklace.[44] And, as promised in "Before the Beginning and After," Surtr burns down the world.

But as Heimdall tells Loki with his dying breath, Loki hasn't won anything. Loki is dying too, but a few are still alive, including Thor's sons, two of Odin's sons, and two humans who took refuge in Yggdrasil's trunk. Balder and Hod return from Hel, and together, they all remake and repopulate the world. The most warlike gods and their biggest threats destroy each other, leaving peace and renewal in their wake. Snorri tempers this a bit by claiming that there are still bad places left; oath breakers and murderers will live in Nastrandir, and the dead will go to Hvergelmir to be gnawed on by Nidhogg.[45] But the earth, Midgard, will be green again with a new sun, and the people will tell stories about the old gods.

Gaiman's ending, though it follows the broad strokes of the Eddas, puts more emphasis on the chess set Balder finds after the battle and its implications. The *Völuspá* and Snorri mention golden checkers in passing as something that survived the fire, but Gaiman puts faces on these pieces. Hod and Balder find tiny golden Odin and Thor, Balder and Frigg, Loki and Surtr. There are enough to make a full chess set, which they arrange on a board and begin to play. On the very last page, Gaiman has only a single line: "And the game begins anew."[46] Myth is a cycle, he implies. We turn back to the first page to hear the stories again, gods pitted against each other in battle over and over.

While Gaiman has stuck broadly to the stories as told in the Eddas and some of the sagas, he has made some obvious adjustments. Where possible, he's beefed up the role of women and played down some of the more problematic elements of their portrayal in the myths.[47] For example, in "The Apples of Immortality," Gaiman gives Idunn a much bigger speaking part, and thus more characterization, than Snorri does. She comes off as sweet but naive, falling for one of Loki's tricks and being kidnapped by a giant. In the *Skáldskaparmál,* Idunn is moved about the story like a chess piece, never speaking for herself or showing any initiative. In the *Lokasenna,* Idunn is portrayed as a peacemaker, which matches the sweet version in Gaiman; while Loki is verbally abusing the other gods, Idunn calms Bragi, reminding him not to attack someone during a feast. Loki then turns on her, accusing her of marrying her brother's killer.[48] Idunn remains calm, and Loki moves on to a new target.

Likewise, Freya is given much more dialogue, which is appropriate considering how often she is treated as a prize or bargaining chip in the gods' dealings with the giants. Gaiman adjusts Freya's characterization by removing implications that she's promiscuous. In "The Master Builder," Freya is outspoken about the deal; the builder, after all, wants the sun, the moon, and Freya in marriage in exchange for building the wall. She argues that they shouldn't trust Loki to make any deal, and she spends the entire story absolutely furious at her circumstances. Likewise, in "Freya's Unusual Wedding," a giant holds Mjolnir hostage and demands Freya's hand in marriage. Despite Thor's thinking that it's just one hand and she has two, so maybe she'll be OK with that, she is, again, furious that they would consider exchanging her for something. Gaiman adjusts the dialogue; in the *Poetic Edda,* Freya declares, "You would know me to be the most sex-crazed of women / if I drive with you to the land of giants."[49] According to Carolyne Larrington, that's the joke: Freya had a reputation for being sex crazed, and her denial was played for laughs.[50] In the *Lokasenna,* Loki accuses Freya of having had sex with everyone in the hall, including her brother.[51] In Gaiman, Freya turns the focus on Thor and Loki instead: "What kind of person do you think I am? [. . .] Do you think I'm that foolish? That disposable? That I'm someone who would actually marry an ogre just to get you out of trouble?"[52] Instead of ironic reinforcement of Freya's reputation, Gaiman leans on Thor's cluelessness for the humor in the scene.

In a similar vein, Gaiman takes advantage of slight differences between the stories in the two Eddas to avoid distinctly problematic overtones. The most obvious example of this is in "The Story of Gerd and Frey," in which Frey is punished for using Odin's high seat, which allows him to see everything in all nine realms, by being lovestruck by a giantess, Gerd. He sends a servant, Skirnir, to ask her to marry him, and Skirnir agrees—in exchange for Frey's magic sword, which is why he doesn't have it at Ragnarök. In the *Prose Edda*, and in Gaiman, Gerd immediately agrees to marry Frey. In the *Poetic Edda*, Gerd refuses Frey's gifts and his proposal, so Skirnir threatens first her life, then her father's; next he threatens her with a lifetime of abject misery, which takes him eleven stanzas to detail. At that point, Gerd agrees to marry Frey. When someone sent a message on Tumblr to complain that Gaiman had "turned the story of Skirnir's Journey into a throwaway couple of paragraphs," Gaiman responded that he'd had the choice between "the longer, poetic rapey version of the story and the prose non-rapey version, and [he] chose the shorter, but non-rapey version."[53] This example is emblematic of Gaiman's overall approach to the stories, keeping to the Edda versions as much as possible but making executive decisions about certain storytelling elements that may prove harmful or problematic to a modern audience.

CHAPTER NINE

Odin and Low Key and Shadow

American Gods

American Gods has been described variously as a road trip novel, a mystery, a postmodern fantasy, a mythopoeic novel, and an epic. Gaiman describes it as "a thriller, and a murder mystery, and a romance, and a road trip."[1] It is dense, sprawling, heavily intertextual, and philosophical. Yet at its core, it is Norse mythology, partially adapted and partially appropriated to bring the ethos of Ragnarök into the modern world and to question Odin's part in it. It borrows from and complicates Western early medieval and medievalist structures and ways of thinking, ultimately examining Gaiman's sense that America has a unique magical foundation that rejects the very idea of gods.

American Gods tells the story of Shadow Moon, an ex-con recruited by Mr. Wednesday, the American version of Odin, to help him gather the old gods—those from ancient cultures, transplanted into America and mostly forgotten—to fight for relevance, worship, and a place in the minds of Americans against the new gods—Media, Technical Boy, Mr. World. What Shadow discovers, however, is that Wednesday is working with Mr. World/Loki to pit the two sides against each other in a battle that will kill most of the old and new gods—and make Wednesday and Loki powerful again. In a purposeful anticlimax, Shadow stops the war and denies Wednesday and Loki the energy from it.

In *American Gods*, Gaiman balances medievalism with purposeful antimedievalism. On the one hand, he centers an early medieval mythology; the text can be read as a morality play, with Shadow pulled between the binaries of old/new, good/evil, life/death. On the other hand, Gaiman pulls mythology into the modern era, updating the gods, fuzzing binaries, and rejecting the Romantic medievalist viewpoint that the Middle Ages were realer and more stable than modernity.

American Gods is an ambitious book, taking on mythologies from around the world and throughout history as it explores the nature of human belief and the American immigrant experience; it invites readers to question what they know about history and the stories America tells about itself. In doing so, it centers Norse mythology and the structure of the Eddas as they lead up to Ragnarök while questioning the very nature of storytelling, especially nationalist storytelling. Rather than using medieval epics or mythology as a foundation to argue that modern life is terrible, or that one nation is better than another, Gaiman crafts a narrative that fractures national identity while showing the continuity of human experience throughout history.

NORSE MYTH IN AMERICA

The theme of *American Gods* is immigration, including how the kind of constant immigration and colonialism the continent has seen for several hundred thousand years affects its mythological makeup. In Gaiman's fictional America, there are no truly native peoples or gods, only imported ones, and they all eventually die out. "This is a bad land for gods" is a phrase often repeated throughout the novel, used to explain why the old gods struggle to keep belief and thus power. America is inherently nonmagical, Gaiman argues, noting that "many folk stories, when they got to America, lost their magic. The magic fell out. There was a weird practicality that came in."[2] The only way it made sense for Gaiman to have magical creatures and gods in America was if they were imported.

The arrival of the Norse pantheon to the North American continent is the second side story appearing in *American Gods.* These stories are ostensibly taken from the journals of Mr. Ibis, the American version of Egyptian god Thoth. He's been recording histories and stories of the gods, how they arrived, and what they are doing, and excerpts punctuate *American Gods.* A group of Norsemen arrive in the general area of Newfoundland in 813 CE; they worship their gods, sing songs about them, and ultimately sacrifice a native to Odin. They're attacked by the natives and massacred, but the gods remain and are present when Leif Erikson arrives a hundred years later.[3]

Just as Ragnarök is the center of Gaiman's *Norse Mythology,* it is the (more obscured) center of *American Gods.* As literature scholar Jorunn Joiner points out, *American Gods* is less an adaptation of Norse myth and more an appropriation; Gaiman uses the mythology but clearly doesn't feel bound by it. Joiner writes, "*American Gods* picks out themes or certain iconography from Ragnarök, and reimagines them in a plot that is apocalyptic, but which treats the apocalyptic as a theme rather than a specific narrative."[4] Readers unfamiliar with the details of Norse myth can still appreciate the plot, but those who know how the myths progress from creation to Ragnarök may have a deeper understanding of Gaiman's structure.

In chapter 8, I argue that Gaiman's Odin knows that Ragnarök is coming, as well as the signs that will presage it, and that this Odin may be read as actively working to bring it about. In *American Gods,* this moves from interpreted subtext to actual text. Wednesday and Loki/Mr. World (whom Shadow knows from prison as Low Key Lyesmith) work together to instigate the war between gods—all of them, not just those of the Norse pantheon. It's a stripped-down, Americanized version of Ragnarök, but it emphasizes an idea about gods that Gaiman introduced as early as *Sandman:* gods are "patterns," "wave functions," "repeating motifs."[5] Wednesday seeks to begin a war because he is Odin, and Odin, Loki, and Ragnarök are inextricably linked.

As an American version of Odin in an inherently nonmagical land, Wednesday has to rely more heavily on cunning than godlike power.

Naturally he becomes a confidence man. Despite the long history of scams—perhaps as long as humanity itself—the idea of the confidence man is quintessentially American, likely because the first man to be termed such was an American operating in New York City.[6] Wednesday spent a long time running classic cons; he tells Shadow about the Fiddle Game and the Bishop Game in great detail on one of their roadside diner stops. At the same time, he's charming the waitress—literally. Shadow sees him drawing runes in spilled salt on the table, reminding the reader that while Wednesday is a much-reduced version of Odin, he's still Odin.

The trajectory of the two-man con run by Wednesday and Loki/Mr. World follows, in broad strokes, an interrupted Ragnarök. It begins with Shadow Moon's conception; we learn in a sequel novella, "The Monarch of the Glen," that his birth name is Balder, and he learns late in the novel that Wednesday is his father. The plan stalled when Shadow's mother took him out of the country and spent most of his childhood traveling, but Wednesday and Loki saw an opportunity when Shadow was arrested and sent to prison. When Shadow is released, Wednesday closes in.

The precursors to Ragnarök in the Eddas include a prolonged winter known as Fimbulwinter, as well as the disappearance of the sun and moon. These signs appear more subtly, cloaked by metaphor, in *American Gods*. The first god Shadow meets is Mad Sweeny, the Americanization of Suibhne mac Colmain from medieval Irish literature. At Wednesday's instruction, Sweeny shows Shadow how to pull coins out of the air and gives him a gold coin to keep. Shadow puts that coin in his dead wife Laura's grave, and later Zorya Utrennyaya, the midnight sister, tells him that he "had the sun in [his] hand" but he threw it away.[7] She shows him how to take the moon out of the sky, and he keeps the moon's coin, in the guise of a silver Liberty dollar, for most of the book. During his time in Lakeside, Shadow deals with deep cold—a particularly bad winter that almost kills him at least once. The removal of the sun and the moon from their rightful places, as well as a hard winter, are the signs of Ragnarök on a smaller and less magical scale—fitting for a less magical America.

Although Wednesday visits a few gods early on, his quest truly begins at the House on the Rock, at a mechanical fortune-teller's. Like Odin visiting the seeress in the *Völuspá*, Wednesday declares that every quest begins with a consultation with the Norns, and he drops a coin in the machine. He doesn't tell Shadow what his fortune says, and we as readers never learn either. Considering how short Shadow's is, it's unlikely that Wednesday gets as much information from the machine as Odin does from the seeress.

In *Norse Mythology*, Gaiman notes that in the time between the stories and Ragnarök, the gods are sleeping. Wednesday spends most of *American Gods* waking them up. The old gods have become complacent and dispirited, doing what they can to scrape by. The first interlude shows this in detail. Bilquis, formerly the queen of Sheba, has become a sex worker in order to glean the worship and power that used to be freely given. Yet when Wednesday approaches them, the old gods don't want to fight. They don't see the new gods as a true threat, and they worry that if it comes to a fight, they might lose what little power and influence they still have. Kali sees through Wednesday immediately, noting that he's clearly only interested in his own glory. Mortals are forgetting the new gods even more quickly than they forgot the old, she says, and this new batch will wane and fall away like the gods of the railway.

To prove to the old gods that the new gods truly do mean them harm, Wednesday and Mr. World collude on Wednesday's ostensible capture and murder. This has two outcomes: the previously reluctant old gods are furious and agree to go to war, and Shadow must keep his prior promise and hold Wednesday's vigil, which is a trap set to kill Shadow in Wednesday's name, thereby providing Wednesday with the power of Shadow's willing sacrifice. Just as Balder's death is the catalyst for the events that lead to Ragnarök in the Eddas, so Wednesday means for Shadow's to be a catalyst for his war. "There's power in the sacrifice of a son," he tells Shadow, "power enough, and more than enough, to get the whole ball rolling."[8] Not only does this statement explain to Shadow what his place in the whole con has been but it also indirectly questions Odin's role in the myths. In visiting the seeress and Angrboda, he learned about Balder's death, Loki's binding, and Ragnarök, but did nothing to stop them. Gaiman implies, through Wednesday, that Odin also sacrificed his son to purposefully bring about Ragnarök.

Wednesday's plan backfires for a number of reasons. He and Loki arranged for Laura's death to sever Shadow from any connections to the world, but Laura didn't stay dead, instead actively interfering in Wednesday's plan and killing Loki. Death isn't insurmountable for Loki or Wednesday, but Shadow also stops the battle that would have restored them, thus foiling their plan and leaving them weakened—technically dead, but death doesn't mean the same thing to gods as it does to humans. Wednesday intended Shadow to play the Balder role, but although Shadow is Wednesday's son, he isn't Balder himself, and he doesn't follow Balder's path. Balder stayed dead; Shadow comes back to life, aided by the gods he's helped and made friends with on his journey. Every choice Shadow makes throughout the novel undermines Wednesday's great plan.

Wednesday is attempting to rig the game and cheat the pattern. His plan is for all—or most—of the gods to die in battle, while the power from their deaths comes to him and the power of the battle's chaos goes to Loki. But what he seems to have failed to realize (or ignored) is that Odin and Loki both die at Ragnarök, and while the world is reborn and goes on, it does so without them. Wednesday is trying to cheat not only all the gods, old and new, but the pattern of mythology itself. *Of course* it doesn't work.

After the abortive battle, Shadow notes that the storm has cleared and the air is "fresh and clean and new," much as the earth is renewed after Ragnarök.[9] The rest of America seems to feel it as well; Sam Black Crow notes that "everything just feels suddenly good right now. Maybe it's just spring coming a little early. It was a long winter, and I'm glad it's over."[10] Even Czernobog feels it. When Shadow arrives to make good on his promise to allow Czernobog to hit him in the head with his hammer, the old god is on the cusp of transforming into his lighter half, Bielebog. "It has been a long winter, boy," he tells Shadow. "A very long winter. But the winter is ending now."[11] After Ragnarök comes renewal—as the *Poetic Edda* notes, "coming up a second time / the Earth from the ocean, eternally green."[12] Wednesday's battle might have been a small-scale, failed Ragnarök, but it built up metaphysical tension that releases when the battle is abandoned.

American Gods is a dense, complex, and heavily inter- and transtextual novel, but the core structure owes a lot to the Eddas and the trajectory of Ragnarök. At the same time, Gaiman does not insist on following the beats of Ragnarök's story, rather borrowing major themes and structures to build his own story around. As Joiner puts it:

> In an act of appropriation rather than adaption, the narrative releases the myth from its historical bonds and brings it, through the genre of fantasy, into the modern United States. There, it is opened up and deconstructed to reveal universal themes of doom and dying gods, and then reconstructed to contain enough iconography to make the myth recognisable in a new format.[13]

Some familiarity with Norse mythology is necessary to fully understand the plot of *American Gods*, if only because Wednesday is a central figure, and his past as Odin strongly informs his role in the novel. But deeper familiarity allows for a richer reading experience, as is so often the case with inter- and transtextuality. The surface level of a war that's really a two-man con is a satisfying plot on its own, but recognizing the echoes of Ragnarök and how those echoes call into question the motives of the original Odin and Loki is even more satisfying.

....

BINARIES, ARCHETYPES, AND MORALITY PLAYS

In *American Gods*, Gaiman returns to the structure of the medieval morality play (discussed in chapter 1). *American Gods* also uses allegorical personification, an everyman figure, and conflict between the allegories over the everyman figure, plus throws in some lessons. However, because *American Gods* is highly postmodern, the binaries are fuzzed, and the lessons don't fall along clear religious or moral lines.

Gaiman's use of gods and god figures in his fiction frequently leans on the idea that they are externalizations of human needs, feelings, and understanding about the world, as discussed in chapter 8. Atsula, wise woman of a nomad tribe from 14,000 BCE, realizes this late in her life: "Gods are great," she says. "But the heart is greater. For it is from our hearts they come, and to our hearts they shall return."[14] Shadow frequently asks gods and god figures if they are real; Bast explains that they are "symbols—we're the dream that humanity creates to make sense of the shadows on the cave wall."[15] The old gods have history and actual names, while the new gods still carry their literal ones—Media, Technical Boy, the car gods.

Gaiman again uses the divide of language and mischief to differentiate between the old gods and the new. The old gods are serious, tending toward heavy speeches and deep insights. Mr. Ibis in particular enjoys pontificating, whether it be at Shadow or through his journals. Shadow thinks of him as a college professor who communicates through "gentle, earnest lecturing," a man who doesn't talk so much as "discourse, expound, explain."[16] Wednesday is also prone to grand statements about the nature of the world, though his tend more toward the shocking or scatological. "Liberty," he proclaims, for instance, "is a bitch who must be bedded on a mattress of corpses."[17] The speech acts of the old gods have history behind them, a weightiness, that the new gods lack.

The new gods, Shadow notes, speak in clichés. At the very least, their threats and offers are shallow and flashy. Technical Boy threatens, multiple times in a single conversation, to kill Shadow for the nebulous offense of "fucking with" him. Media, in the guise of Lucy Ricardo, offers him money and sex. The Spooks, personifications of a shadowy government agency, act exactly how you'd expect them to if you've watched *The X-Files* or *The Bourne Identity*, playing good cop/bad cop and using aggressive questioning techniques. Their very modernness echoes Nowadays and New Guise from *Mankind*.

Shadow serves as an everyman figure whom the gods fight over, much like the angels/morals and demons/vices do in morality plays. He is a generalizable human, a man of uncertain ethnicity and of no religion in particular. People frequently ask if he's part Native American or Black. The Starz TV adaptation (2017–21) cast Ricky Whittle, a Jamaican British mixed-race actor, to visibly portray this ambiguity. Early on, he has no real internal drive or meaning; as writer and literary critic Rut Blomqvist notes, Shadow accepts things at face value, follows orders because orders are meant to be followed, and does what Wednesday tells him to because he has no internal drive of his own—at least at first.[18] In Lakeside, he takes on a name so generic as to be self-referential: Mike Ainsel, which Klinger notes is a bastardized version of "me a'an sel," or "my own self."[19] Even when Shadow begins to try to act for himself, Wednesday has manipulated him so cleverly that he still does what Wednesday wants: holding Wednesday's vigil and offering himself as a willing sacrifice. Shadow is the character through whom the audience learns about the world, the old gods and new, and the lessons conveyed.

Morality plays are heavy on binaries, and at first *American Gods* seems to be too. Wednesday tricks everyone into believing that there is only room for one set of gods in America—only room in the human heart and mind for only one of tradition or modernity. We can have the messy roadside-attraction authenticity of a purportedly real America, or we can have the glitzy, shallow, essentially inauthentic world of technology and media. In the end, Shadow realizes that these binaries are false. There is no true difference between the old and new gods; similarly, America is made up of multiplicities, not a monomyth. Shadow himself occupies multiple, often liminal, positions throughout the novel. For example, he is on parole, so he is not in prison but not truly free; he is married, but his wife is dead—although not really; he is human but divine; he is dead yet lives.[20] If there is a binary in *American Gods*, it is in Wednesday's attempt to reduce the vast multiplicity of America to a new monomyth: just him and Loki.[21] Of course this fails.

Though Gaiman makes postmodern the structure of the morality play, *American Gods* does still carry lessons—a moral, if you will—about the nature of stories, how humans tell them, how humans fit ourselves into them, and how America in particular tells stories about itself. Mr. Ibis claims, "The important thing to remember about American history [. . .] is that it is fictional, a charcoal-sketched simplicity for children, or the easily bored."[22] America is far more complicated than the stories accepted as history express, yet history and America itself seem to smooth out all the complications. America "tends to eat other cultures," Gaiman has said; in America, "everything homogenizes, everything blands."[23] Through Shadow's experiences, *American Gods* pushes back both on "bland collectivism" and complete individuality.[24] Shadow says he's happier being a human than a god because humans can live without other people believing in them, but his whole journey has shown that people do still need other people to believe in them and support them to survive and thrive. We are individuals, yet we need each other, and we need things to believe in.

Another philosophical argument in *American Gods* is that being human is to believe in things. Shadow is urged to believe "everything," and through Sam Black Crow, he sees what that looks like. She gives him a lengthy speech about the various and contradictory things she can and does believe in, "things that are true and [. . .] things that aren't true and [. . .] things where nobody knows if they're true or not."[25] By the end, Shadow realizes,

> People believe. [. . .] It's what people do. They believe. And then they will not take responsibility for their beliefs; they conjure things, and do not trust the conjurations. People populate the darkness; with ghosts, with gods, with electrons, with tales. People imagine, and people believe: and it is that belief, that rock-solid belief, that makes things happen.[26]

Literary critic Ray Bossert reads the gods as tools, ones that humans create and use as needed, only to abandon when times no longer call for those particular tools.[27] Gaiman explores what happens to them when people stop needing them, much as books like Margery Williams's *The Velveteen Rabbit* (1922) or films like *Toy Story* (1995) have done. Americans in particular, Gaiman notes, abandon their tools faster than other people; his explanation is that there's something about the continent itself that rejects magic, gods, and belief.

ANTIMEDIEVALIST MEDIEVALISM

By leaning on Norse mythology but also pushing back against the monomyth, Gaiman ends up with an interesting antimedievalist medievalism in *American Gods*. Many fantasy novels romanticize the Middle Ages, casting them as a time/place of simplicity and magic, but *American Gods* pushes back against the idea that humans and nations have ever been simple, that there's any clear divide between past and present, and that modern life is somehow less authentic than premodern life.

Medievalist texts often portray the Middle Ages as more real and stable than modernity—yet at the same time more magical. The idea that technology drove out magic, that the industrial revolution killed the fairies, has a long history. Likewise, as author and scholar Siobhan

Carroll notes, the foundational authors of contemporary fantasy, such as J. R. R. Tolkien, resist the very sort of "blanding" that Gaiman notes in American culture—a blanding they see as endemic and inevitable in industrial modernity.[28] Wednesday uses this idea to pit the gods against each other. He argues that the new gods, "gods of credit-card and freeway, of internet and telephone, of radio and hospital and television, gods of plastic and of beeper and of neon,"[29] are fundamentally incompatible with the old-world mythologies represented by himself, Czernobog, Anansi, and Kali. Carroll points out that readers are primed to go along with this interpretation of the situation because Wednesday's argument "mesh[es] with readers' expectations of the genre."[30] But *American Gods* isn't just fantasy; like America, it contains multitudes. Wednesday's insistence on past/present, old/new, and them/us dichotomies is shown to be false, part of the con. Instead, Gaiman argues for a continuity of metaphysics: magic, science, and gods are all fundamentally products of the human imagination. The new gods are just as real as the old gods, and all of them can be forgotten, relegated to the museum-like room Shadow visits in his first dream.

Gaiman argues that America's past is a story—a heavily edited and simplified one. It calls into question every nationalist epic from the *Aeneid* to the Eddas to the Arthurian mythological cycle. Such epics—traditional stories, often poems—help establish the past of a nation or community, and in so doing, they create an origin story for the in-group or nation. They're also often used to justify or legitimize the authority of the ruling class; for example, Arthurian legend has been used to establish a (fictional) continuity from pre-Roman Britain through Elizabethan England, arguing for the right of various groups and kings to rule over the British Isles.[31] Comparative literature scholar Susan Gorman argues that *American Gods* is a "postmodern epic," one that, instead of presenting a unifying history of the United States, shows how fractured the history truly is: "there are many histories, both of America's people and their gods."[32] Mr. Ibis's argument about American history being written for children is one part of Gaiman's point, as is Wednesday's declaration that the only thing holding America together is a shared landmass, currency, and popular culture. As Gorman puts it, "*American Gods* shows how much the national past is a story, crafted and continually revised."[33] If that is true of American history, of course it is also true of the rest of history, including the prettied-up (or dirtied-up) versions of the Middle Ages that populate contemporary medievalist thought.

CHAPTER TEN

"Eating, Drinking, Killing, and Fornicating"

Robert Zemeckis's *Beowulf*

Beowulf is one of the most famous poems in Old English, a 3,180-line epic about a man fighting monsters—and so much more. *Beowulf* tells the story of a hero who travels from Geatland to Denmark to rescue a tribe of Danes from a marauding monster, then must also kill the monster's mother. After returning home, he continues to fight for his own king, then becomes king himself, fights a dragon to protect his kingdom, and dies. The simple plot's multiple themes, both culturally specific and universally human, run throughout the poem. Between its use of language and its themes, so much remains for academics to unpack that books, articles, and dissertations continue to be written about it.

Despite not being a work purely by Gaiman, as most of the texts explored in this book are, this is easily one of the most densely medievalist texts.[1] Not only does this version of *Beowulf*, a film written by Neil Gaiman and Roger Avary and directed by Robert Zemeckis, depict a medieval world that conforms more to the modern audience's expectations of the medieval than to the true medieval, but it also projects modern issues and anxieties onto this faux medieval world and generalizes them. Modern worries about politicians more concerned about their own fame, glory, and pleasure than being effective leaders are used to attack the very idea of heroism, which is never questioned in the poem. Modern concerns about male sexuality and men's inability to control themselves coalesce into an origin story for monsters previously lacking one; these monsters go on to attack and decimate entire communities. Modern ideas about storytelling and how stories are passed on are raised in the film, with explorations of unreliable narration ranging from the personal to the cultural to the historical. The Middle Ages become a time of magical possibilities that absorb all of our current concerns, anxieties, and cynicism. At the same time, the filmmakers are aware of what is required to make a marketable product, but one that is also in conversation with the larger academic idea of Beowulf. These competing forces lead to a tension within the film and in its marketing materials as the filmmakers attempt to present their *Beowulf* as cooler than the poem, yet accurate and worthy of academic attention. It's a fascinating cross section of medievalism; it is fascinated and repulsed in equal parts by the Middle Ages and the idea of *Beowulf* as a high-culture artifact.

....

INTRODUCTION TO *BEOWULF*

Beowulf survives in a single damaged manuscript that collects several Old English poems and stories, many of them dealing with monsters or monstrous behavior, earning it the moniker Monster Manuscript.[2] The manuscript itself is only a small part of the history of the poem; as Old English and medievalism scholar Chris Jones notes, our understanding of *Beowulf* begins in medias res, since the written-down version of the poem (c. 1000 CE) is unlikely to be much like the orally delivered original.[3] Much scholarly ink has been spilled over the poem, who wrote it, and when it was composed, not to mention how this might apply to a written poem derived from an orally delivered "original." Scholars have argued that the poem is originally Danish, written by a scop around 340 CE, and was translated by an English monk. Others argue that it is an original English poem written around 650 CE. Some argue for a single author, and others for a series of ballads combined later into a single work. A few scholars suggest that the poem was the work of a nun rather than a monk; Hild of Whitby has been floated as a potential author. Arguments still break out over early dating (between 500 and 700 CE) and late dating (between 900 and 1000 CE). All that is known for sure is that someone wrote down a poem around 1000 CE. We have no way of knowing what the story was like before then or when it was initially composed; nor do we know who composed it or who the audience was.

The critical history of *Beowulf* follows much the same trajectory as that of Norse mythology: mostly ignored until the early 1800s, then appropriated as a national epic to help cement legitimacy and history, as the *Iliad* was seen to do for Greece and the *Aeneid* for Rome. The English weren't the only ones to claim *Beowulf*, however. Scholar and translator R. M. Liuzza points out that the poem was "claimed by the English (because of its language), the Danes (because of its subject), and the Germans (because of its setting in the pre-Christian north)."[4] For about a hundred years, the work was treated as archeological and anthropological, not as a work of art, with scholars attempting to mine it for information about northern and early English culture. Many sought to reach past the Christian interpolations to find the original pagan poem; some even argued that the character of Beowulf was an updated version of Freyr, one of the Norse gods. Even when the critical approach to the poem shifted to treating it as art, heated arguments between so-called paganists and Christianists continued well into the 1900s.

This was the state of the field when J. R. R. Tolkien wrote his famed "*Beowulf*: The Monsters and the Critics" (1936). He takes to task the dominant critical approach, pointing out that attempting to use the poem as a historical guide and then judging it for being a bad one is wrongheaded. He argues that *Beowulf* is primarily art, and good art, but that critics' tendency to think that medieval people were inherently less intelligent and unlearned prevents them from accepting that a medieval person could compose something good. He also chides them for assuming, because of their beliefs about the general intelligence level of medieval people, that the *Beowulf* poet would be unable to separate Scandinavian myth and Christian doctrine, and thinking that that is the reason the poem has such a blend of both.[5]

In the mid-twentieth century, more attention was paid to translations and editions, which made the poem accessible to those without access to the British Library. Beginning in the 1960s, New Criticism was brought to bear on the poem, focusing on its inherent meaning, allegory, and religious framework. Other critical theories and approaches followed.[6] Then, in 1999, Irish poet Seamus Heaney produced a translation/adaptation of the poem, and *Beowulf* exploded into popular culture. As academic E. L. Risden notes, the popularity of "Heaneywulf" told capitalism that there was money to be made.[7] The floodgates—such as they were—opened.

....

REWRITING *BEOWULF*

Between the years 1999 and 2007, at least five Beowulf films were released: Graham Baker's *Beowulf* (1999), *The 13th Warrior* (1999), *No Such Thing* (2001), *Beowulf and Grendel* (2005), and Robert Zemeckis's *Beowulf* (2007). Varying widely from sword-and-sorcery heroic epic to sci-fi horror, the films have one major thing in common: a tendency to use *Beowulf* as a starting point and focus on modern issues rather than strictly adapting the poem. Three of them (*13th Warrior*, *Beowulf and Grendel*, and Zemeckis's *Beowulf*) purport to tell "the story behind the story," offering explanations of varying degrees of plausibility for the events in the poem. All the films are medievalist in their own way, but the "true story" approach that insists on some level of untold historical accuracy puts these three, and especially Zemeckis's *Beowulf*, firmly in the medievalism camp.

The medievalism of Zemeckis's *Beowulf* is twofold. On the one hand, the film presents a medieval-coded world, with lip service paid to an idea of authenticity. On the other, the filmmakers have taken the poem apart, looking for a different story inside it, and put it back together in a way that makes it modern. Both of these are common for medievalist texts and media, especially film. Medievalist films have a documented tendency to blend realism and fantasy, to treat the Middle Ages as a "supernatural rather than real period" of history,[8] as a site of fantasy in opposition to the "reality" of the present.[9] At the same time, a film's attempts at authenticity are used to boost the prestige of that film, but what authenticity means is often more about what audiences expect than any adherence to historical realism. As medievalismist Bettina Bildhauer puts it:

> Audiences will enjoy a film more if it looks authentic to them, if they can imagine the stories told to have really happened, and especially if they can have this confirmed by experts. However, they will also enjoy a film more if it offers a satisfying artifice with a star adding contemporary or monumental grandeur, beautiful images and exciting narratives—features that draw attention to its filmic nature rather than simulate transparent access to the past.[10]

Zemeckis's *Beowulf* does both, with varying degrees of success. The early Middle Ages setting—507 AD, as the opening splash tells us—is presented in a traditionally barbaric way, with overindulgent Danes and attention drawn to bodily functions. Yet the film itself is CGI over motion capture, leaving no room for belief that it is anything but a film—a spectacle, not an authentic look back into a realistically represented Middle Ages. While Zemeckis claims that the CGI presents a "more real" experience, it is firmly in the camp of Jean Baudrillard's concept of hyperreality, playing on the mind's inability to separate real and simulation, especially as technology advances to the point that simulation appears more real than reality.[11]

Medieval films also have a noted tendency to strive for the origins of stories—the story behind the myth—as part of their realism and

Zemeckis's *Beowulf* film opens with barbaric debauchery and an establishing splash of "Denmark AD 507."

authenticity.[12] Often they will appeal to academic authority, as in Antoine Fuqua's *King Arthur* (2004), whose opening splash informs us that "historians agree" that the Arthurian myths are based on real people and that "his true identity" has been indicated by "archeological evidence."[13] There is, of course, no such archeological evidence and no such consensus by historians. The film, however, presents a believable Dark Ages time frame with a notable lack of magic, knights, grails, and other Arthurian staples, leaning instead on the history of the decline of Rome in Britain. Similar origin stories or otherwise ahistorical presentations of history can be seen in medievalist films such as Ridley Scott's *Robin Hood* (2010) and Mel Gibson's *Braveheart* (1995).

Beowulf thus fits neatly into an established genre of films and medievalist approaches to the Middle Ages and medieval stories. Unlike *Beowulf and Grendel* or *The 13th Warrior*, it leans into magic and monsters rather than rationalizing them away, portraying the medieval as "a place of fantastic possibility."[14] Despite, or perhaps because of, the date stamp of "Denmark 507 AD," the setting is magically ahistorical, using the Middle Ages as a time and place where magic can be believed to exist.

Yet the filmmakers pointedly do not believe in their own source material. This approach—that the scribe who wrote down *Beowulf* was lying to us—is easily the most fascinating part of Avary and Gaiman's process, eagerly seized on by Zemeckis. In *Beowulf, the Script Book*, Avary notes that as he read *Beowulf* in high school, he began to doubt the veracity both of the story and the scribe: "Perhaps scenes had been added to spice up the tale. And perhaps, as I increasingly suspected, critical elements had been left out, edited by the passage of time." The questions raised by what he perceived as "gaps" in the narrative "all seemed to add up to rather nefarious conclusions."[15] Those conclusions were that Hrothgar was Grendel's father and Beowulf was outright lying about his fight with Grendel's mother.[16] But Avary still couldn't get the dragon to fit—until Gaiman suggested that if Grendel was Hrothgar's son, then the dragon must be Beowulf's. Avary refers to it as "the Beowulf Unified Field Theory."[17] Yet there's a disconnect in the way Avary and Gaiman respectively talk about the story. On the one hand, Avary seems to believe he's "fixing" it, putting back in all the "not ready for prime time" material he believes must have been edited out by Christian monks. Gaiman, on the other hand, approaches it as he does any story: material for the compost heap. "The glory of *Beowulf* is that you are allowed to retell it," he says in one of the DVD special features. "And I think that's the power of these old stories. It's still the same story."[18] Their *Beowulf* film is just another way of telling the story, not an attempt to reach into an inaccessible, nonexistent past to restore a poem ruined and censored by Christianity.

Zemeckis seems outright gleeful at the idea of fixing *Beowulf*, which he declares, frequently, to be "boring" and "uninspiring." He blames this on its age and its authorship.[19] He finds Gaiman and Avary's version better because it "has nothing to do with the *Beowulf* that you were forced to read in junior high school. It's all about eating, drinking, killing, and fornicating."[20] Instead, he claims, the writers "put back in" the stuff they thought the monks had removed, and as a result, there was more excitement—not to mention more sex. As Sylvia Kershaw and Laurie Osmond put it, "Zemeckis's *Beowulf* presents itself not as an adaptation of the Anglo-Saxon poem, but as a creative rediscovery of emotional and psychological truths that have been obscured by the original source."[21] Zemeckis is fully behind the idea that somehow, by reading between the lines, Gaiman and Avary have accessed the lost oral tradition and produced a version of *Beowulf* that is more real and authentic than the extant copy available to us.

This is, of course, nonsense, but it has its roots in the history of *Beowulf* scholarship. The search for an original and more authentic pagan poem was long a popular trend in medieval studies. In particular, the Christian material was viewed with suspicion, and repeated attempts were made to excise it, either by finding an extant pagan poem that could be pointed to as the inspiration for *Beowulf* or by dividing it into discrete sections—the folk songs thought to make up the story before the monks glued them together with overtly Christian themes.[22] Only in the early 1900s did scholars begin to admit, then to accept, that the text's Christianity is integral to the poem as we have it, and no extant work can be pointed to as the original. Instead, the author was a Christian person writing about a pagan time from within his own perspective and for his contemporaries, borrowing from the histories and myths of pre-English Germanic cultures and Christian theology.[23] While Zemeckis's and Avary's preoccupation with the original, oral pagan poem behind the written version is much more about plot and character truths they believe were hidden by prudish scribes, their "story behind the story" approach isn't that much different from these early scholars'.

They do not, however, miss that there is a clear push and pull between paganism and Christianity in the poem, and they adapt this tension to screen—to an extent. The poem frames the Danes' and Geats' paganism as a tragedy, showing that although they are noble, they are technically worshiping demons (Odin and Thor) and asking them to save them from another demon (Grendel).[24] The film shows the Danes on the threshold of the conversion to Christianity, portraying both religions as equally useless, but Christianity as the more sinister of the two. The representative of "this new Roman god" is Unferth (John Malkovich), who repeatedly beats his slave, challenges Beowulf's claims to heroism, and is accused of fratricide and his murdered brothers of incest.[25] By the second half of the film, with Christianity well entrenched, Beowulf laments that its doctrine of pacifism is destroying his own values: "The time of heroes is dead. [. . .] The Christ-god has killed it, leaving humankind nothing but weeping martyrs and fear and shame." Rather than a "tension" built on a Christian viewpoint looking back at a pagan era, the film puts the two religions directly at odds "in terms of a Christian passivity and pacifism and a robust and militant paganism."[26]

This view of Christianity is fairly typical for medievalist films. As medievalist Christopher Roman explains, Hollywood frequently sets up Christianity as a monolithic, antagonistic force and film heroes as "caught between institutional conformity and a primal relation to nature that represents freedom."[27] There is no compromise available between the hero and the church; if conflict arises, the hero always dies rather than integrate. Beowulf's values are in direct conflict with those of Christianity; he is a warrior, a larger-than-life fighter, a hedonist. He doesn't die in direct conflict with Christianity or the church, but he does die because of his own values and as a consequence of his own actions—actions that Unferth refers to as "the sins of the fathers."

The religious conflict in the film is a deliberate choice on Gaiman and Avary's part; if they were attempting to tell a true story of Beowulf, one with any kind of claim to historical accuracy, they could easily have left Christianity out entirely. The Scandinavian nations did not begin converting until the eighth century, two hundred years after the setting of *Beowulf* in AD 507. Likewise, portraying it as a weak, pacifistic religion in opposition to the warlike Norse doesn't quite jibe with early English Christianity, which celebrated martyrs who died heroically and framed Christ as a warrior battling death itself.[28] Rather than showing any interest in the history of the conversion of northern Europe and England, the filmmakers project modern beliefs and attitudes about the church backward onto the Middle Ages—which is part of the core definition of medievalism.

Attitudes about Christianity are not the only modern anxieties projected onto the Middle Ages in Zemeckis's *Beowulf*; most of the changes to the plot and themes come from the tendency to project these anxieties. Zemeckis's *Beowulf* is, of course, not alone in radically altering the plot of the poem for a film version; in many ways, this *Beowulf* is more faithful to the source text than any of the preceding films—at least as far as the plot is concerned. None of the filmic versions of the story has truly captured the themes of the poem, possibly because those themes are alien enough to a modern audience that Hollywood would never take a chance with them. These themes include ideas particular to Germanic heroism, such as the characteristics of a good king and how they conflict with the characteristics of a good warrior, and how their tribal society was structured and a person's duties within it. Some behaviors presented as virtues look like vices to modern audiences, such as boasting, which was necessary to establish one's identity and strengths.

Zemeckis's *Beowulf*, like Baker's *Beowulf* and *Beowulf and Grendel*, rejects the black-and-white, hero-versus-monster morality of the poem. Instead, it raises the monsters closer to humanity and reduces the heroes closer to monsters. Avary and Gaiman don't go quite as far as Mark Leahy and David Chappe, the screenwriters for Baker's *Beowulf*, who overtly presented Beowulf's parentage as demonic; he is the son of a human woman and the demon Bael. But neither is their Beowulf the unimpeachable hero whose biggest mistake was creating a peace so long-lasting that nobody but he had the skill to fight a dragon.

Instead, he is a lecherous, boastful, glory-hungry liar, embodying the presumed unreliable narrator that Gaiman and Avary found in the poem to begin with. It's worth noting that medieval literature doesn't have any such thing as an unreliable narrator as a narrative device, and assuming one is another form of medievalist backward projection, taking a (post)modern concept and applying it to a medieval text. Gaiman has noted this assumption to be a "post-modern habit" of his.[29] The film is deeply distrustful of the very idea of heroism, changing Beowulf's accomplishments into empty boasts at best and outright lies at worst.

The ideas of heroism and monstrosity represent one of the disconnects in theme between the poem and the film brought on by a radical shift in cultural and literary values. The poem's Beowulf is somewhat more than human; he has the strength of ten men in one hand, and he can hold his breath underwater for hours. The poet uses the word *æglæca* to refer to Beowulf, the dragon slayer Sigemund, Grendel, and Grendel's mother. The word has confounded translators because of this usage, and it has been variously translated as "monster" and "awe-inspiring," depending on whom it's being applied to.[30] This does not mean, however, that Beowulf and the monsters he fights are the same; Beowulf fights monsters and saves people, with no ambiguity about where his morals and loyalties lie. The films consistently blur the line between hero and monster, and Zemeckis's *Beowulf* in particular equates them, with Grendel's mother claiming Beowulf is "as much a monster as my son, Grendel." The only difference, she argues, is that Beowulf has "glamour," whereas Grendel looks like a monster.

Monsters in stories serve to externalize threats, but modern film and literature tends to reinternalize them; we have met the monster, and he is us. The monsters in Zemeckis's *Beowulf* are threats that the Danes posed to themselves. In the film, Hrothgar fathered Grendel, a monster whose physical deformities included an exposed tympanic membrane. Then the Danes were extremely inconsiderate neighbors, singing too loudly in their celebrations, which drove Grendel into a frenzy. Once Beowulf arrives and kills Grendel, Grendel's mother avenges Grendel's death. Then Beowulf repeats the cycle by fathering the golden man/dragon with Grendel's mother. Some of this is the result of an obsession with origins; the films want to explore where the monsters came from and why they're attacking, but the poem needs no such explanation—they are monsters, and they are there to be defeated by the hero.[31] Providing the monsters with a backstory makes them more sympathetic, which reduces sympathy for the heroes who kill them. But Gaiman and Avary go further, making the heroes frankly antiheroic and showing a general mistrust of heroes and heroism that is firmly rooted in the twenty-first century. Kershaw and Osmond note that the film "encompasses both a sincere desire for the triumph of heroes and death of monsters, and an anxious sense that the heroes themselves exceed the roles required of them."[32] The heroes, such as they are, inflict the monsters on their own people, and the physical monsters are merely the result of the true monster: unchecked male sexuality.

In Zemeckis's *Beowulf*, sex and men's inability to (or lack of desire to) resist it are the causes of all the problems in Heorot. Grendel, who attacks Heorot and slaughters the Danes, is revealed to be the son of Hrothgar. He is Hrothgar's only son because his much younger wife, Wealthow, refuses to have sex with him because of his liaison with Grendel's mother. This opens the door for Beowulf to become Hrothgar's heir and marry Wealthow after Hrothgar dies by suicide, but Beowulf falls prey to the same temptation as Hrothgar. His vulnerability to sexual temptation is foreshadowed early in the film, when he tells the story of his swimming match against Brecca. He argues that he only "lost" the swimming match because he was attacked by sea monsters, but it is revealed that one of the sea monsters he supposedly fought was actually a siren who seduced him. Likewise, he is openly attracted to Wealthow and makes no pretense otherwise, even in sight of Hrothgar and his entire court. He shows little resistance to Grendel's mother, and in the third act, fifty years later, he is shown keeping an enslaved girl as a bedmate; it's implied that she is merely the latest in a long line of them. Wealthow is just as disgusted with Beowulf as she ever was with Hrothgar, though she has a bit more respect for him. However, Beowulf also doesn't have a legitimate heir, which is the same problem Hrothgar had; Wiglaf takes over for him after his death. The cycle appears poised to repeat itself yet again when Grendel's mother appears to Wiglaf at the end of the film. The "male-sexuality demon," as Risden puts it,[33] not only destroys the individual lives of the men but the entire community.

Many scholars and critics have tackled the question of why film adaptations of *Beowulf*, particularly Baker's and Zemeckis's, have insisted on adding so much sex, and they have come up with several equally plausible explanations. Risden suggests that the filmmakers think audiences wouldn't be interested in a purely heroic epic, or that sexuality is so embedded in twentieth- and twenty-first-century American culture that you can't have a film without it. He also suggests that the addition of so much sexuality comes from a cultural homophobia, a need for the hero to demonstrate "appropriate masculine drives."[34] Kathleen Forni and Nickolas Haydock both point to the sociopolitical landscape of the time, noting that "great men" being brought low by sexual scandals was in the zeitgeist; as Haydock puts it, "the notion that adultery and lies about adultery could enfeeble a powerful man had an especial salience."[35] Critics Andrew Osmond and Roger Ebert suggest that it's to appeal to an audience of "bloodthirsty boys"; despite the lack of actual nudity, Ebert says, "If I were 13, Angelina Jolie would be plenty nude enough for me in this movie, animated or not."[36] Essentially they argue that the over-the-top sexuality, not to mention the naked fight scene frequently compared to a comedic one in *Austin Powers* (1997), is a lowest-common-denominator appeal to less-than-sophisticated audiences. Whatever the impulse, Risden argues, adding sex and sexuality "reshapes the story as a fable largely about the problems of the male sex-drive."[37] Women, in contrast, are either helpless bystanders (Wealthow, Ursula) or monstrously sexual predators to this particular male weakness (Grendel's mother).

ACADEMIA, POP CULTURE, AND STUDY GUIDES

Scholars have long argued about the ways that Beowulf films in general and Zemeckis's *Beowulf* in particular get it wrong, pointing out errors in everything from themes to plot to architecture and weaponry. A medievalist reading of the film, however, is less concerned with pointing out errors (although that can be fun) and more concerned with why these changes were made—what they tell us about our modern anxieties and values. Like any adaptation, *Beowulf* is as much a translation as are actual translations of the poem; it must be accessible to its contemporary audience. Haydock argues that academic analysis and criticism of the poem has always projected modern ideas back onto the text,[38] and even Heaney's wildly popular translation contained clear modifications to match his own politics.[39] Likewise, Jones points out that the filmmakers "have no duty to treat the poem authentically," even if such a thing was technically possible.[40] The medievalism of the Zemeckis *Beowulf* is most visible not only in the modern ideas applied to a medieval text but also in how it approaches academia.

The *Beowulf* filmmakers' relationship with the poem and by extension academia is fascinating. Gaiman seems to have treated the whole process like any other adaptation, retelling the story in an interesting way and not as competition for or a replacement of the poem. Avary loved the poem but found it riddled with flaws, raising questions that he decided he had the answers to. Zemeckis hated the poem, yet he declared that the adaptation "should stir some debate in academia."[41] What sort of debate he expected is unclear, but if he thought that Gaiman and Avary's explanations for the "holes" in the story would be taken up by medieval scholars as plausible, he's probably disappointed. The poem connotes the worst of academia—stuffy, old, elitist—but it also provides name recognition and a level of authority that the filmmakers attempt to capitalize on. In promotional materials, the poem is constantly invoked and frequently conflated with the film.

Nowhere is this more obvious than the lesson plan package released by Young Minds Inspired, a company that describes itself as "a full-service educational marketing agency that specializes in developing and distributing customized outreach programs for corporations, associations, non-profits, and government agencies."[42] The packet for *Beowulf*, commissioned by Paramount, includes several lesson plans and activities. It uses the poem—"an epic that has been passed down for centuries though oral storytelling, written verse, and now film"[43]—as a legitimizer for the lesson plans and exercises, which themselves are based on the characters and plot as seen in the film, not as portrayed in the poem. Each page is branded with the film's title and production companies' logos, and the lessons themselves encourage seeing the film in theaters—but never suggest reading the poem.

Yet academic concepts and thought patterns bleed over into the film; besides the search for a pre-Christian version of the poem in both academia and the screenplay discussed above, there are also noticeable, if simplified, concepts from feminism and gender studies in the film. Jones notes that the film provides a view of what academic scholarship looks like from the outside: "the film is a record of what escapes the academy and how its various discourses are selected, edited, altered, understood, misunderstood, and re-understood."[44] Haydock sees it differently, arguing that this is the very reason academics dislike films like this—"not because they ignore advances in scholarship but because of how they reflect them: we feel misunderstood and misappropriated."[45] As with so many modern adaptations of classical (or otherwise academic) works, there is a clear tension between pop culture and elitism that infuses the film and its meta- and paratextual surroundings.

Zemeckis's *Beowulf* and the attitudes and culture surrounding it are a microcosm of a larger ongoing discussion about historical accuracy in modern medievalist media and how essential it is (or isn't) to represent the Middle Ages as they were, especially in fantasy texts. The film also specifically reflects Beowulf studies, however inadvertently, with its attempts to return to a pre-Christian version of the story while also approaching it with a modern mind-set and projecting modern ideas and anxieties onto the text. It is ultimately a fascinating collection point for ideas and attitudes about medievalism, medieval studies, and the academy.

CHAPTER ELEVEN

Where Shadow Meets Grendel

Beowulf, "Bay Wolf," and "The Monarch of the Glen"

Hollywood production being what it is, the screenplay that would become Zemeckis's *Beowulf* began to be drafted twenty years before the film came to theaters. In the meantime, Gaiman wrote two more pieces using *Beowulf* as inspiration.

"Bay Wolf" (1998) was the result of several forces, not least of which was people frequently mishearing Gaiman when he said he was working on a *Beowulf* screenplay and thinking he was working on the popular TV series *Baywatch* (1989–2001).[1] "Bay Wolf" is a two-hundred-line narrative poem that places Larry Talbot, a werewolf character Gaiman created for an earlier story, in the role of Beowulf in a futuristic, hedonistic Los Angeles.[2] The drug and party kingpin of Venice Beach, Gar Roth, calls Talbot to deal with a creature that's killing his clientele and damaging his business. Talbot discovers Grand Al, a monster who lives in the wreckage of an oil rig with his mother, is the culprit and kills him—but maybe not the mother. The poem follows the basic plot of the first half of *Beowulf*: Grand Al terrorizes Venice Beach; Talbot arrives to help; Talbot tears off Grand Al's arm and chases him back to his lair, where he meets Grand Al's mother; he then returns to Gar Roth for his reward. The poem also nods to the screenplay: Grand Al's trouble is that the parties are too noisy, and Talbot refuses to reveal whether he killed or had sex with Grand Al's mother.

"The Monarch of the Glen" (2004) is a novella set in the American Gods universe, which, along with "Black Dog" (2015) and a promised third novella, serves as a bridge between *American Gods* and its anticipated sequel novel.[3] In it, Shadow Moon continues his travels through Europe and the United Kingdom, ending up in Scotland. He's hired to act as additional security at a private party for incredibly rich people, but it turns out that his true role is fighting a monster in a conflict described in cosmic, mythological terms. Shadow refuses to kill the monster; instead, the rich people burn to death in the manor house. Grendel's mother declares that Shadow is under her protection, and Shadow leaves Scotland for London and eventually Chicago.

As with most medievalist texts, "Bay Wolf" and "The Monarch of the Glen" borrow from and allude to medieval literature but present modern concerns. These two stories in particular do not project these concerns backward onto the Middle Ages, which is a common medievalist structure; instead, they broaden, generalize, and mythologize *Beowulf* in order to use its structure and monsters to discuss them. Nor do these pieces present as a direct retelling of *Beowulf*; instead, they appropriate it. Gaiman uses recognizable bits of the poem to make the allusions clear, but he abandons anything unnecessary to get his own themes across. In this case, the use of medieval literature is less like a compost heap and more like Tolkien's soup pot, with recognizable figures and story structures periodically boiling to the top, to be used (mostly) intact. Unlike the film, these *Beowulf*-inspired stories don't present as a version of the early English story; rather than attempting to retell or directly adapt the poem, "The Monarch of the Glen" and "Bay Wolf" use the idea of monsters and nods to the characters of the poem to explore issues of mythology, monstrosity, and class conflict.

MYTHOLOGIZING BEOWULF

Although *Beowulf* has its roots in mythology, the poem itself isn't properly a myth. Joyce Lionarons, medieval scholar and author, notes that myth is defined by its independence from any inter- or intratextual dialogue; myth is timeless and authorless, and because of this, it is wide open to interpretation and reuse.[4] Medievalist and *Beowulf* translator R. M. Liuzza classifies it as "neither myth nor folktale," too bound up with its "complex background of legendary history" to be easily defined as either.[5] Similarly, medievalists and linguists R. D. Fulk, Robert Bjork, and John Niles classify *Beowulf* as three "folktale-like episodes" embedded in historical and cultural commentary.[6] *Beowulf* is often boiled down to the three monster fights because those are the most generalizable parts of the story. The legendary history, the frequent and lengthy digressions, and the opening that discusses a king who dies before the story even starts are all important to the story the poet was trying to tell and important to the point they were trying to make, but they no longer resonate with or even make much sense to a modern audience thanks to shifts in social structures and values.

Instead, modern writers who take on *Beowulf*, including Gaiman, keep the focus on the immediate narrative of the poem—the fights with Grendel, his mother, and the dragon. The importance of these battles becomes unmoored from the context around them as they are rewritten for a modern audience, as we saw in chapter 10. Kershaw and Ormond argue that this focus on narrative and its subsequent unmooring "allows Gaiman to transmute the medieval poem into the stuff of myth—where myth is understood as something which speaks to aspects of the human psyche that are seen as elemental and therefore unchanging."[7] The characters of the poem become archetypes—hero, warrior, monster, hag, dragon—and the themes generalized to the human experience.

"Bay Wolf" has more obvious *Beowulf* influence than "The Monarch of the Glen" in that it follows the basic beats of the Grendel fight. But instead of an adaptation, Gaiman gives us a pastiche—*Beowulf* by way of Baz Luhrmann, with a protagonist originally written for a Lovecraft-style short story collection.[8] The *Beowulf* influences are meant to be immediately recognizable, yet "Bay Wolf" is divorced from

Beowulf in setting, tone, and character—a Californian beach instead of a Scandinavian mead hall, the horror-film destruction of pretty young people rather than the dismembering of adult warriors, a drug kingpin obsessed with money and rival gangs rather than a king trying to hold his tribe together. What remains is a "hero" fighting a monster who travels from his home in an undesirable location—the mere for Grendel, an abandoned oil rig for Grand Al—nearly killing him, then following him back to his lair to deal with his mother. Thematic material that is generalizable to the human condition remains visible in "Bay Wolf"; Gar Roth keeps asking if it's rival gangs or the mafia attacking him, echoing the tribal warfare and feuding of *Beowulf.*

"The Monarch of the Glen" further divorces these archetypes from the poem, much as *American Gods* divorced Wednesday from Norse mythology. Shadow is manipulated into fighting a monster, an unnamed, bald young man/creature. This fight is framed as Beowulf versus Grendel, but it is also couched in cosmic, mythological terms; it is one battle in the eternal war between man and monster, us versus them. Mr. Alice tells him the fight is about keeping the monsters, the "them," down, because humanity has already won: "We were the knights, and they were the dragons, we were the giant-killers, they were the ogres. [. . .] They know their place now. And tonight is all about not letting them forget it."[9] It is a ritual fight, Mr. Alice explains, rather than one truly about protecting the group. The rich people lure the monster out of the loch by deliberately provoking him with loud noises, then set Shadow on him. It seems hyperbolic when Mr. Alice says it, but during the fight itself, Shadow feels it:

> This fight was old, Shadow thought, even older than Mr. Alice knew. [. . .] It was the fight of man against monster, and it was old as time: it was Theseus battling the Minotaur, it was Beowulf and Grendel, it was the fight of every hero who had ever stood between the firelight

> and the darkness and wiped the blood of something inhuman from his sword.[10]

Shadow dreams of Wednesday before the fight, and Wednesday also invokes Perseus and Rama. Perseus is from Greek myth; he is the son of Zeus and a mortal woman, killed Medusa, and rescued Andromeda from Cetus. Rama is a Hindu god, one of the avatars of Vishnu, associated with night, delight, and beauty. His stories tell of a lengthy but ultimately successful war against demons. In this way, heroes from multiple mythologies are held up as parallels; they too protect all of humankind from outside forces, represented in all these stories by a singular monster—Grendel, Medusa, the Minotaur, Shurpanakha. All of them are divorced from their context to stand as archetypes of the hero against the monster.

Enough of the story elements remain to justify comparing Shadow's fight to Beowulf versus Grendel; people gather in a manor home, they have a party, and the Grendel figure attacks the partygoers. Shadow refuses to fight him with a weapon, instead wrestling him barehanded.[11] Shadow's Grendel is taken back into the loch by his mother, and Shadow leaves Scotland. (The Grendel and Grendel's mother analogs in "The Monarch of the Glen" are unnamed in the text, so I refer to them as such here.) These details, along with the common additions or changes Gaiman tends to make, align "The Monarch of the Glen" clearly with Beowulf rather than any of the other hero-versus-monster stories invoked in the novella.

As with *American Gods*, the point of "The Monarch of the Glen" isn't to be a true adaptation of *Beowulf*. Rather, Gaiman uses the idea of Beowulf as an intertextual evocation of man versus monster. Shadow once again becomes a disruptive force in the way things purportedly should go. Just as he disrupted an attempt at Ragnarök in *American Gods*, now he disrupts a ritual that kept the old gods out of the United Kingdom.

At the end, Shadow comes down on the side of the monsters, upending centuries of tradition and balance.

MONSTROSITY VERSUS HEROISM

Much like Zemeckis's *Beowulf*, "Bay Wolf" and "The Monarch of the Glen" are laser focused on questions of monstrosity and heroism. Talbot, as a werewolf, is undeniably a monster, and identifies as such: "Hey, I'm not a monster / Not your monster, anyway / Not yet," he tells Gar Roth's men when he arrives.[12] The opening line of "The Monarch of the Glen" is Gaskell's remark that Shadow is "something of a monster."[13] In both cases, defining the protagonist as a monster is a prelude to sending them to fight another monster. In doing so, both stories raise purposeful questions about who exactly is the monster here, and who is merely reacting to aggression or perceived aggression. Monsters are about their culture; as theorist Jeffrey Jerome Cohen puts it, "The monster is difference made flesh, come to dwell among us."[14] The monster is the other, an embodiment of the differences between people or aspects of ourselves we don't want to acknowledge; it is unable to be defeated or killed. These differences or aspects rely on the surrounding culture; a culture constructs its monsters in ways that uphold existing power structures.[15]

As discussed in chapter 10, *Beowulf* is far less ambivalent about monsters and heroes than its modern-day adaptations and appropriations tend to be, but it is fairly typical in that it uses monsters to represent problems with society or human nature. Both of Gaiman's works fuzz the monster/hero binary; in so doing, they make literal these societal or human problems. In *Beowulf*, Grendel represents the threat of family strife and destruction of the Danes—a destruction that the poet foreshadows in the early parts of the poem as an internal threat as well as an external one.[16] Grendel's mother has been assigned many meanings over the couple hundred years' worth of *Beowulf* criticism, but her attack on Heorot is often seen as justified according to Scandinavian and early English terms of feuding. Beowulf killed her son, so she kills Æschere, one of Hrothgar's warriors. She thus represents feuding and the endless back-and-forth of attacks and counterattacks that mark a feud. Collectively, the monsters and other mythical elements of *Beowulf* represent the work required to maintain civilization in a culture beset with violence from without and within—and, ultimately, its failure.[17]

In "Bay Wolf," the young people who come to Gar Roth's parties are self-destructing even before Grand Al arrives; Gaiman calls them "dusted, shot up, cranked out," noting that Grand Al leaves "steroid-shrunken testes" behind on the beach after one of his kills.[18] Grand Al is likely able to wreak as much havoc as he does precisely because everyone is constantly high—inattentive and incautious—which makes them easy pickings. Likewise, the incredibly loud music they play covers up the screams when the victims are attacked. Naturally Gar Roth never considers shutting down the party to save his people. He calls in Talbot instead.

Gaiman uses several techniques to sway the reader's sympathies toward Grand Al and away from Gar Roth while keeping Talbot fairly neutral. Gar Roth is a drug kingpin, a criminal who pays off the police to keep his perpetual party going. Gaiman establishes the music as entirely too loud early on, with Talbot commenting on it multiple times, both in narration and in dialogue; at the end, he tells Gar Roth that Grand Al was just a neighbor tired of their noise. The first on-page deaths are a pair of young people, and the imagery of the attack clearly alludes to both *Jaws* (1975) and *Creature from the Black Lagoon* (1954). Both films involve humans invading the territory of a nonhuman creature, which attacks and kills them as invaders, although through no real fault of its own. These allusions, in addition to assisting the reader with mental images of the incident itself, align Grand Al with a pair of monsters who only attack when humans are in their territory. When Talbot fights Grand Al, the only indication of how it's going comes from Grand Al's dialogue: "And he said, *What are you?* / He said, *Ow, no, ow.* / He said, *Hey, shit, this isn't fair.*"[19] This, again, serves to increase sympathy for Grand Al, to reduce his monstrosity, though it doesn't fully eliminate it. After all, Grand Al is still killing people, ripping them to pieces, and leaving the pieces all over the beach.

Talbot, despite taking the place of Beowulf in the action, is by definition a monster; he is an immortal werewolf who wants nothing more than to die. In the first story he appears in, "Only the End of the World Again," he is shown vomiting up a child's fingers and a dog's paw, remains of victims from the night before.[20] He takes the job killing Grand Al not because of Grand Al's threat to the human population but because he's being paid. He doesn't tell Gar Roth about Grand Al's mother, and it's quite likely that he hasn't killed her either. At the end, he gives Gar Roth one word, "Danegeld," referring to the tribute paid by the English to the Vikings to prevent raids. His intention is unclear; he may simply mean that with the threat removed, Gar Roth owes him his fee, or he may be extorting him, subtly threatening similar attacks on the beach if Gar Roth fails to pay him. His earlier remark that he's not "your" monster, "not yet," increases the threat behind his words. Beware setting a monster to hunt a monster.

In "The Monarch of the Glen," a similar inversion of hero and monster plays out. Nearly everyone in the story is framed as some sort of monster: Gaskell calls Shadow, Grendel, and Grendel's mother monsters; Gaskell is a child murderer; Jennie is a *hulder* (a Norwegian forest creature);[21] and Mr. Smith, Mr. Alice, and the rich folks at the party are also monstrous. Narratively, however, Shadow stands somewhere between hero and monster: Grendel and Grendel's mother present as practically human and clearly care for each other, and Jennie is bound by her nature, though she mostly wants to go home. The nonhumans—or nominally human; Shadow is technically a demigod—are far less monstrous than the story's humans.

Shadow's nature is the focus of a great deal of "The Monarch of the Glen." He is pulled between various forces, all of which want something from him. Gaskell, Smith, and Mr. Alice want him to be a hero-monster, someone who will fight their fight and then die. Mr. Alice tells Shadow he's a hero, but Shadow knows Mr. Alice thinks of him as a monster: "But you think I'm *your* monster," he thinks, in an echo of Talbot.[22] He dreams of the Norse gods, who beg him, "Bring us back or let us go."[23] Shadow tells them multiple times that despite his birth name and parentage, he's not their Balder, but at the end, he finds that his actions have freed them. In his dreams, Wednesday tells him that Shadow's not a hero either; because he's died and come back, he no longer fits the archetype. Jennie wants him to fulfill the role of the Lover in her folktale, then ultimately tells him he's not a man. If the only options are man, hero, or monster, then that leaves Shadow as monster. He refuses to identify as such, mostly because he has different ideas of what monsters are than Gaskell or Alice do.

The ostensible monsters of the story, the nonhumans who carry the label, are mostly harmless. The *hulder* Jennie helps out at the bar, tries to warn Shadow to leave town, and saves him from certain death. Grendel and Grendel's mother act like a perfectly normal mother–son duo, right down to her cleaning his face with tissue and spit. Grendel doesn't attack until he's provoked, and even then, he doesn't kill anyone. Grendel's mother offers her protection to Shadow when Shadow refuses to kill her son. Their only monstrousness is being on the "them" side of Mr. Alice's equation; they are not human, so they must be eliminated.

If one defines monstrosity by one's behavior rather than one's nature, then the clear monsters in the story are the humans. Gaskell claims everyone's a bit of a monster, including himself, but Shadow dreams/discovers that Gaskell murders little boys and takes pictures of their bodies. In "Keepsakes and Treasures," a previous story Smith and Mr. Alice appeared in, Smith is shown to be a murderer and pedophile, while Mr. Alice uses his extreme wealth to purchase an "exotic" sex slave. The horde of unnamed rich people provoke Grendel out of the loch, force Shadow to fight him, and then try to beat both of them to death. Shadow recognizes that this is part of the ritual; both monster and hero must die. But Shadow refuses to die and refuses to kill, and in the chaos of his disruption of the ritual, the manor house catches fire, and all the rich people die in the blaze.

While the *Beowulf* poet embodied and externalized internal or cultural threats to the Danes and the Geats, Gaiman breaks down the boundaries between us and them to question just who is a monster and who gets to decide who is a monster. Talbot is a werewolf, he has killed and eaten people, and he works for a man whose business model leads to lots of dead people—but in killing Grand Al, he prevents more deaths. Shadow is not quite human, a demigod, a resurrected dead man, and someone who sides with the monstrous nonhumans and destroys a centuries-long ritual to protect Britain from these monsters and outside gods—but the nonhumans aren't actively hurting anyone, and the humans are. Gaiman once again makes postmodern a traditional narrative and its traditional conflict by blurring the boundaries between us/them, monster/hero, and native/outsider.

CLASS CONFLICT

While both "Bay Wolf" and "The Monarch of the Glen" set up the central conflict as ostensibly between different types of monsters, with one being a bit more heroic than the other, an undertone of class conflict also runs through both—more explicit and clear in "The Monarch of the Glen" but still subtextually present in "Bay Wolf." Kathleen Forni has noted that British authors in particular use *Beowulf* adaptations or appropriations to set up themes of the common versus the elite, or an underdog versus the immense power of certain cultural forces (money and power, the media, foreign armies).[24] Although *Beowulf* is almost entirely about the elite—earls, kings, and their thanes—it too shows internal societal conflict through external monsters. Where "Bay Wolf" and "The Monarch of the Glen" deviate is by introducing overt class consciousness to the insider/outsider dichotomy.

Talbot is a working-class hero, coded as a noir-style detective or hit man. Gar Roth is filthy rich; "he owned the world, from Laguna Beach north to Malibu," and his version of Heorot is a beach hall built for a nonstop drug-fueled orgy.[25] He expects that his opponents have the same status he does; he suspects the Israeli mafia or the Chinese. But Grand Al isn't a rival at that level; he lives in the remains of an oil rig, rusted and abandoned, alone with his mother. He is, as Talbot puts it, "a neighbor" who "wanted you to keep the noise down."[26] Forni reads the plot as "the revenge of the original inhabitants of a beachside neighborhood on the obnoxious partying of the criminal nouveaux riche."[27] The poem, short as it is, manages to work in condemnations of gentrification and tourist towns—again subtly invoking *Jaws* in Gar Roth's refusal to close the beach to stop the killings.

In "Bay Wolf," the rich win; Talbot kills Grand Al and returns the beach to its usual too-loud partying. This is partly a side effect of Gaiman following the expected beats of *Beowulf*, because "Bay Wolf" is an adaptation of the original poem. The same cannot be said of "The Monarch of the Glen," which provides flexibility in how Gaiman takes on the theme of rich versus poor in the novella. The clearest sign that the story is at least partially about class conflict is in the title itself; the story shares a title with a well-known painting from the Victorian era, one romanticizing the elite sport of hunting. Forni notes that this sport was often at the expense of the common folk, as the gentry appropriated huge tracts of land for hunting estates, preventing the common folk from using that land for anything else.[28]

Gaiman establishes the unnamed Scottish town near Cape Wrath as a poor, isolated one. Jennie refers to it as a "fucking graveyard" and says while they "feed on" tourists, there's never enough of them.[29] The hotel is the only business Shadow interacts with, and the food and service are terrible. The town brings to mind Lakeside in *American Gods*, but without the kobold protection; Gaskell fills the role of quirky, tale-telling man with a dark secret, but he's just a man, not a supernatural guardian. Jennie may be supernatural, but her associated folktales only give her the power to protect one man, not allow an entire town to thrive while others around it fail.

Elite tourism is again a target in "The Monarch of the Glen"; a horde of extraordinarily rich people descend on the town. In this case, they don't even bring their tourist dollars and boost the local economy. Instead, they set up outside town and bring in all their own food and labor. Shadow is the only local hired, although they have no intention of paying him; they expect him to die. Their sport is provoking, then killing, a heretofore harmless local—one who just happens to be an undefined nonhuman—as well as the hero they lift up to fight the monster.

The sudden brutality of the rich people, after all the talk of cosmic, preordained battles and protecting humanity, is where the literal truth shows through, with the rich and elite actively preying on the poor and ostensibly weak. This demonstrates and makes literal the violence inherent in the system, so to speak; the oppression and exploitation of the poor by the rich manifest in their attack on Shadow. However, Shadow, as a disruptive force, flips the script, refusing to kill Grendel and calling for help from Jennie. Whether it's her help or his refusal to complete the ritual that causes it, the bonfires explode, and the rich people all die. Shadow returns Grendel to his mother, who notes that he might be hurt, but at least he's not dead, "and that makes a nice change."[30]

Smith doesn't think it's a nice change—not only because now he has to pay Shadow but also because of all the work it will take him and his employer to clean up the mess; they have to create plausible reasons for the deaths of so many of the "great and the good."[31] Yet despite all these deaths, it doesn't seem that Shadow's actions have had a lot of impact on the physical state of the world. The only named rich person, Mr. Alice, is so rich that he can be essentially invisible; as Smith explains in "Keepsakes and Treasures," "There are people out there who are being paid more than you will ever see in your life to make sure you never hear a breath about Mr. Alice on the telly or in the papers."[32] He is truly in charge of all the machinations that led to this point, and he left before the chaos started. Thus, the highest of the elite are completely untouched—for now.

In both works, Gaiman uses class as a marker of the monstrous, but he overturns the usual fantasy politics of the elite as strong protectors and instead leans on more modern, liberal, even Marxist themes of elite abuse of the poor. "The Monarch of the Glen" in particular draws attention to the ways that the elite use the "manipulation of myth to sanction or justify the power of the privileged."[33] By using the title of the painting—which appears only briefly in the story—Gaiman makes explicit that these themes were included on purpose and are central to the story itself. The rich in these stories are the cause of their own troubles, and those troubles overflow onto those beneath them socially.

....

"BAY WOLF" AND OLD ENGLISH POETICS

I would be remiss if I failed to draw a bit of attention to the poetry of "Bay Wolf" and the ways it echoes *Beowulf* and other Old English poetry. Let me begin with the opening of the poem; the first word is "Listen" as Gar Roth explains the problem to Talbot. A few lines later, Talbot's narrative voice shifts that order to the reader: "Now you listen."[34] "Listen" is, of course, one of the many ways that the opening word of *Beowulf*, *hwæt*, has been translated.[35] Gaiman doubles it, first using it to grab attention—Talbot's, with "listen," and ours, with the rest of the line: "Somebody's killing my people"—and then bringing readers in as Talbot speaks directly to them.

Gaiman also uses puns and double meanings, albeit with a heavier hand than the *Beowulf* poet;[36] in one case, these puns even slide over into something resembling a kenning. In describing a party, Talbot refers to the girls as "popping fearmoans and whoremoans," playing on "pheromones" and "hormones" while also establishing the noises the girls make, of both fear and desire.[37] Later, Talbot jokes with Grand Al that he's "one of the avaunt guard," moving from *avaunt* (go away) to *avant-garde* (new or experimental).[38] Plays on words such as these are also visible in *Beowulf*, though they will likely go unnoticed by casual readers because they don't translate well into modern English. However, a few make it through the language barrier; for example, after Beowulf's defeat of Grendel, Hrothgar orders the hall to be "folumum gefrætwod"—decorated or adorned by hands—at which point Grendel's arm is hung on the wall.[39] Likewise, during Beowulf's fight with Grendel's mother, there's some linguistic slippage with "ofsæt" that allows for reading her as "setting upon" or "sitting upon" Beowulf; the entire encounter, in fact, is riddled with double meanings.[40]

Finally, Gaiman toys with an appositive structure similar to *Beowulf*'s. Appositives are two words or phrases that describe the same referent in different ways, usually providing more information about that referent. In the case of *Beowulf*, the poet uses appositives in multiple ways, including for contrast and emphasis.[41] For example, as the poet summarizes Beowulf's fight with Grendel to set up Grendel's mother's attack on Heorot, he uses several appositives in a relatively short passage:

> Thus he [Beowulf] overcame the fiend,
> subdued the hellish spirit. He [Grendel] went away wretched,
> deprived of joy, to find his place of death, mankind's foe.[42]

Here, "overcame the fiend" is paralleled with "subdued the hellish spirit," "Grendel" with "mankind's foe," and "wretched" with "deprived of joy." In "Bay Wolf," Gaiman uses appositives that echo Old English poetry twice, once to describe how Grand Al kills—"It took maybe a dozen of them, dragged them into the sea, / death in the early morning"—and once to describe Talbot's boasting—"*That's right*, I told him, tough-talking in the afternoon."[43] While the purposes don't exactly line up with appositives in *Beowulf*, their presence invokes Old English poetry.

In addition to Old English verse in general and *Beowulf* in particular, "Little Red Riding Hood" sounds midway through the poem as Talbot watches Grand Al kill the young couple: "I got sharp ears / *(all the better to hear them with)* and good eyes / *(all the better to see them with)*."[44] As usual, Gaiman has absorbed, borrowed, and blended myth, folktale, fairy tale, and classic literature into his unique style, but enough of the influences retain their shape for readers familiar with them to further appreciate how he builds his poetry on the shoulders of these predecessors.

EPILOGUE

"Make Good Art"

Some Final Thoughts

One constant in Neil Gaiman's work, despite its wide variation in tone and medium, is its clear debt to and usage of everything that came before, from myth and fairy tale to history and sociology. Everything is mulch for the compost heap, ingredients for the soup pot. Some of it comes back out in recognizable chunks, while some is fully composted, providing themes and atmosphere rather than direct references. Yet his work isn't clichéd or derivative; his use of his antecedents is purposeful and thoughtful, adding something new to the mix. As author Darrell Schweitzer puts it, "A writer can't merely stand on the shoulders of giants. He has to do something interesting while he's up there. A little tap-dance, maybe. Gaiman does at least that."[1] Recognizing Gaiman's references can be rewarding in itself, but understanding what he's doing with those references, why they're there, and how they reflect or rework his predecessors can be doubly so. The specifically medieval antecedents and medievalism, from the outright to the blurrily refracted, are what I've tried to tease out and examine in this book, but there's much more there.

Because of the sheer volume of Gaiman's output, there wasn't space to get into every work in his oeuvre that utilizes medievalism, and not every work that could be considered medievalist was big enough or had enough medievalism in it to warrant an entire chapter. "October in the Chair," one of his short stories, could be compared to Chaucer's *Canterbury Tales* in a number of ways: it's a frame story featuring several people telling stories to each other, and it includes an instance of someone farting in someone else's face, which calls to mind "The Miller's Tale" specifically. *Odd and the Frost Giants* is another of his Norse mythology books, a historical fantasy about a boy who helps the Æsir take Asgard back from a frost giant.[2] And in "Chivalry," an old woman finds the Holy Grail in a thrift store and haggles over it with Galahad.[3] In the illustrated, stand-alone version of *Chivalry*, artist Colleen Doran purposefully imitates medieval artworks such as the Bayeux Tapestry and illuminated manuscripts.[4] Gaiman cowrote a crossover collection for Vertigo, published in 2015, entitled *Free Country: A Tale of the Children's Crusade,* in which all the children of an English town go missing and are discovered in a magical land called Free Country, where all the children who have ever disappeared, including those on the partially historical, partially apocryphal Children's Crusade of 1212 CE. Even this quick roundup fails to cover every remaining work with any hint of medievalism in it.

Frequently the focus for medievalismists is on direct references to the Middle Ages, be they from writers,[5] politicians,[6] or groups/social movements.[7] Usually the reaction to these references is negative, thanks to some perceived misuse or misappropriation of the Middle Ages. But it can be just as important to explore benign medievalisms—that is, good-faith use and reuse of tropes, themes, and stories from or attributed to the Middle Ages. This kind of benign medievalism is mostly what we find in Gaiman's works. Rather than needing to unpack claims of realism based on what we think the Middle Ages were like, we can instead tease out the layers of inspiration and how interpretations and reinterpretations of medieval material have made their way into Gaiman's work.

Medievalism is also not the only lens we might use to view Gaiman's work. Another lens comprises Jewish beliefs and worldviews. Yet another is social justice, making it possible to examine his work through feminist, queer, class, race, and disability critical frameworks. The sheer amount of his work that is or has been illustrated allows for art criticism as well, including examinations of styles and how artwork affects the meaning of related text. As with any artist, more than one thing is going on, and tracing his influences back to the Middle Ages is just one way of examining his work. So, if at any point in this book, you were like, "Wait, but what about—" then it's likely that unpacking that particular aspect wasn't my point, and I chose to avoid some tangents. In my estimation, these layers of meaning, the multiple possible ways of reading, analyzing, and evaluating a work, the fact that a work will resonate differently with different people—all these are the mark of a good artist.

In 2012, Gaiman advised the graduating class of Philadelphia's University of the Arts to "make good art"—that is, to make art true to yourself, art that is perhaps a bit too personal, that makes you feel like you're "exposing too much of your heart and your mind and what exists on the inside."[8] Gaiman has done this for the last forty years, and one of the things his work reveals is a curious and voracious mind that hoovers up everything in his path, then twists it in delightfully creative ways to present work that is deep, layered, and thoughtful. His chosen set of genres—fantasy and horror—are particularly well suited for this approach, as they are unbound from strict reality and reach into the subconscious and unconscious of individuals and societies.

Art is important, and every piece of art builds on or owes something to an uncountable array of art that went before it. Every generation borrows, redefines, rewrites, and updates existing stories to fit its own cultural needs, and thus refresh and renew them. I hope that this book has introduced you to new, interesting ways of looking at art in general and Neil Gaiman's art in particular. I hope it has piqued your interest in some of his influences, from medieval epics and romances to the Victorian works that built on those epics and romances. And perhaps it has given you a different way of thinking about the Middle Ages and its associated art, as well as how we tell ourselves stories about our histories. After all, humans are storytelling creatures; stories are how we understand ourselves, our world, and each other.

ACKNOWLEDGMENTS

Huge thanks to those who helped by donating books from my wish list so I didn't have to spend hundreds of dollars on them myself: Beth Adams, Jes Battis, Kellyann Fitzpatrick, Merry Harrison, Jeff Hartline, and Paul Sturtevant contributed enormously to my Gaiman research library. Others helped by tracking down sources, recognizing and/or translating obscure bits of text, providing copies of sources I couldn't get myself, and otherwise saving me a great deal of hassle: Brandon Hawk, Aaron Macks, Kristen Noone, Cory Rushton, Erasco Meistersuppe (if that's your real name, Very Helpful Twitter Person), and the social media person for the Archives de Littérature du Moyen Âge. Very special thanks to interlibrary loan librarian Toccara Porter; I absolutely couldn't have done this without the expert help.

Thanks to Zabé for getting this book to a publisher, and to Meredith, Karen, Susan, and Kavita for helping make it the best it can be.

To the Clowder (Alex, Alexis, Andrew, Kianna, Kim, Matthew, Michelle, Ravi, Suja, Vanessa, Varsha, and Will), for the moral support when publishing gets to be a lot, and especially Kim for the chats about sources on fairies and fairy tales. And to the Hive (Beth, Cody, Dani, Emily, Jenny, Jillian, Leah, Marina, and Rhiannon): thanks for the beta reading, the cheerleading, the reassurances that I know what I'm talking about and am kind of smart actually, and the mental health support. I love you all.

And to Eric, who had the idea for this book in the first place.

NOTES

Introduction

1. Gaiman, "The Wake: An Epilogue," *Sandman* 73 (1995), in *Sandman: The Wake.*
2. Sarah Lyall, "Neil Gaiman on His *Norse Mythology*, in Which Odin Wants a Wall," *New York Times,* February 12, 2017, https://www.nytimes.com/2017/02/12/books/neil-gaiman-norse-mythology.html.
3. Dana Goodyear, "Kid Goth: Neil Gaiman's Fantasies," *New Yorker,* January 25, 2010, https://www.newyorker.com/magazine/2010/01/25/kid-goth.
4. Gaiman in Sommers, *Conversations with Neil Gaiman,* 131.
5. Gaiman, "Of Meetings and Partings," 12; Jo Walton, "Something Else Like . . . Roger Zelazny," Tor.com, November 11, 2012, https://www.tor.com/2012/11/11/something-else-like-roger-zelazny/.
6. "Neil Gaiman: The Book I Wish I'd Never Written," interview with Rebecca Hawkes, *Telegraph Online,* May 29, 2015, https://www.telegraph.co.uk/culture/hay-festival/11638724/Neil-Gaiman-The-book-I-wish-Id-never-written.html.
7. Gaiman and McKean, "Neil Gaiman and Dave McKean: How We Made *The Sandman,*" interview with Dave Hoad, *Guardian,* October 22, 2013, https://www.theguardian.com/culture/2013/oct/22/how-we-made-sandman-gaiman?INTCMP=ILCNETTXT3487.
8. Writing a comic is much like writing a film or an episode of television: the writer produces a script, and the artists then produce the art with the writer's guidance.
9. The Will Eisner Comic Industry Awards recognize achievement in American comic writing, art, and editing.
10. The Hugo Awards are highly prestigious because they are voted on by fellow authors. Best related work is awarded to nonfiction, art, and other works that aren't necessarily fiction. *Sandman*'s nomination was for the art in "The Dream Hunters" (1999), a nonsequential story in the Sandman universe illustrated by Yoshitaka Amano.
11. Gaiman, script for chapter 1 of "The Kindly Ones," *Annotated Sandman,* 4:18.

12. Nick Hasted, "Bring Me a Dream," *Independent*, September 5, 1996, https://www.independent.co.uk/arts-entertainment/bring-me-a-dream-1361818.html.
13. Hoad, "Neil Gaiman and Dave McKean."
14. Gaiman, "Sources of Inspiration," MasterClass: Neil Gaiman Teaches the Art of Storytelling, 2019, https://www.masterclass.com/classes/neil-gaiman-teaches-the-art-of-storytelling/.
15. See Janega and Emmanuel, *Middle Ages*, for an informative breakdown of the different dates that bookend the Middle Ages and historians' reasons for using them.
16. Mommsen, "Petrarch's Conception of the 'Dark Ages.'"
17. For more on the problems of historicity, labeling time periods, and the various ways that we misremember the Middle Ages, see Kaufman and Sturtevant, *Devil's Historians*; Albin et al., *Whose Middle Ages?*; Matthews, *Medievalism*; and Pugh and Weisl, *Medievalisms*.
18. Faxton, "Pre-Raphaelite Brotherhood," 55.
19. For a much more thorough and detailed—yet not so detailed it's boring—look at the development of fantasy literature, see Mendelsohn and James's *Short History of Fantasy*.

Chapter One | Sandman and Everyman

1. My discussion contains spoilers for the Sandman comics and only a brief discussion of the Netflix series, which, as of this writing in 2022, only covers a tiny part of the comics. Series watchers should be warned that the comics have notable differences. For graphic novels, I cite the issue number, page number, and panel number, counting panels chronologically. Using this method, this quote comes from *Sandman*, issue 8, page 9, panel 4 (8.9.4). For consistency's sake, I use the *Annotated Sandman* for all numbering. Because the *Annotated Sandman* is black-and-white, discussions of art and color are based on the 30th anniversary trade paperback editions.
2. Lucien, the librarian of the Dreaming, refers to him as "the incarnation of this Dreamtime." Gaiman, *Annotated Sandman*, 2.13.2.
3. Gaiman, introduction to *Sandman: Endless Nights*, 6.
4. Watkins, "Allegorical Theatre," 767–68.

5. King, "Morality Plays," 244.
6. Watkins, "Allegorical Theatre," 771–72.
7. Kolve, "*Everyman* and the Parable of the Talents," 78.
8. *Mankind*, lines 129–34.
9. *Mankind*, lines 142, 144–46.
10. Ashley, "Titivillus," 140.
11. Gaiman, *Annotated Sandman*, 12.10.4.
12. King, "Morality Plays," 242.
13. Watkins, "Allegorical Theatre," 767.
14. Bocharova, "Personification Allegory," 43.
15. The cognitive psychology behind allegorical personification is outside the scope of this discussion but is fascinating nonetheless. For a thorough discussion on the topic, see Melion and Ramakers, *Personification*.
16. Gaiman, *Annotated Sandman*, 1:33.
17. Gaiman, *Annotated Sandman*, 21.18–20.
18. Gaiman, *Annotated Sandman*, 21.11.1.
19. Gaiman, *Annotated Sandman*, 48.16.1.
20. *Summoning of Everyman*, lines 486–88.
21. The phrase comes from part of an ancient collection of tablets and documents, the *Hermetica*. The ideas from the *Hermetica* percolate through ancient and medieval thought, like so much of ancient philosophy did. The full phrase may be translated as follows: "That which is above is like to that which is below, and that which is below is like to that which is above, to accomplish the miracles of all one thing." See Steele and Singer, "Emerald Table."
22. Gaiman, *Annotated Sandman*, 1.20.4.
23. Gaiman, *Annotated Sandman*, 7.4.1.
24. Gaiman, *Annotated Sandman*, 36.19–20.
25. Gaiman, *Annotated Sandman*, 35.7.4, 36.29.4.
26. Gaiman, *Annotated Sandman*, 16.19.3
27. Gaiman, *Annotated Sandman*, 16.23.2.
28. Gaiman, *Annotated Sandman*, 9.14.5.
29. Gaiman, *Annotated Sandman*, 13.23.6–7.
30. Gaiman, *Annotated Sandman*, 13.24.4.
31. Gaiman, *Annotated Sandman*, 69.10.1.
32. Gaiman, *Annotated Sandman*, 69.10.1.

Chapter Two | Crossing the Threshold

1. Gaiman, *Annotated Sandman*, 15.22.2–3.
2. Macrobius, *Commentary*, 81–90.
3. Gaiman, *Annotated Sandman*, 10.5.7–8.
4. Gaiman, *Annotated Sandman*, 10.9–14.
5. "The Doll's House," *Sandman*, season 1, episode 7, written by Heather Bellson and directed by Andrés Baiz.
6. Chaucer, *The Book of the Duchess*, lines 4 and 34–35, in *Complete Poetry and Prose*.
7. "Pearl," line 59, in *Poems of the "Pearl" Manuscript*, Andrew and Waldron, ed.
8. Langland, *Piers Plowman*, line 3.
9. Gaiman, *Annotated Sandman*, 15.3.5.
10. S. Russell, *English Dream Vision*.
11. Spearing, *Medieval Dream-Poetry*, 20.
12. "Pearl," lines 67–96.
13. Spearing, *Medieval Dream-Poetry*, 17.
14. S. Russell, *English Dream Vision*, 6.
15. Guillaume de Lorris and Jean de Meun, *Romance of the Rose*, 334.
16. Chaucer, *Book of the Duchess*, lines 1324–34.
17. Chaucer, *Parliament of Foules*, line 20, in *Complete Poetry and Prose*.
18. Langland, *Piers Plowman*, lines 154–216.
19. Gaiman, *Annotated Sandman*, 16.18.9.
20. This is one of the biggest changes from page to screen. In the Netflix show, Jed is in the company of Gault, a living nightmare who wishes to be a dream. Jed himself plays the role of the Sandman, complete with superhero costume. Lyta and Hector are here part of Rose's story line, and Lyta conceives her child with the ghost of her husband in a dream.
21. Gaiman, *Annotated Sandman*, 1:294.
22. Gaiman, *Annotated Sandman*, 11.4–5.
23. "The Parliament of Rooks" is a one-shot issue released two years after *The Doll's House* wrapped. Gaiman, "The Parliament of Rooks," *Sandman* 40 (1992), in *Annotated Sandman*, 3:20–44.
24. Gaiman, *Annotated Sandman*, 40.2.6.
25. Gaiman, *Annotated Sandman*, 40.21.2–3.
26. Gaiman, *Annotated Sandman*, 40.9.1.

Chapter Three | Abandon Hope

1. In writing his *Divine Comedy* (c. 1308–21), Dante was in no way the first medieval author to craft a travelogue of Hell, Purgatory, and/or Heaven, just the most popular and the longest lived. Consider the case of the twelfth-century *Visio Tnugdali* (Vision of Tnugdalus), in which a sinful knight falls into a deathlike stupor and is guided through Hell by an angel, experiencing punishments along the way.
2. Dante, *Inferno* (trans. Cary), 3:1–9.
3. Gaiman, *Annotated Sandman*, 4.2.1, 4.3.4, 4.19.8, and 4.23.4.
4. Gaiman, *Annotated Sandman*, 1:113.
5. Dante, *Inferno* (trans. Palma).
6. Gaiman, *Annotated Sandman*, 4.6.5.
7. Gaiman, *Annotated Sandman*, 4.6.7.
8. Gaiman, *Annotated Sandman*, 4.6.6–7.
9. "Lani Diane Rich and Alisa Kwitney, "I Am Hope (V1.4–5)," *Endless: A Sandman Podcast*, July 13, 2021, https://endless.transistor.fm/episodes/i-am-hope-v1-4-5.
10. Gaiman, *Annotated Sandman*, 4.7.8.
11. Gaiman, *Annotated Sandman*, 9.13.4–5, 9.17.2, and 9.19–21.
12. In the Netflix version of "A Hope in Hell," Morpheus tells Matthew that Nada "defied" him. "A Hope in Hell," *Sandman*, season 1, episode 4, written by Vanessa Benton and directed by Jaime Childs.
13. Gaiman, *Annotated Sandman*, 1:113.
14. Gaiman, *Annotated Sandman*, 1:121.
15. In the Netflix series, Lucifer is played by Gwendoline Christie, a female actor, and no pronouns are ever used for Lucifer in dialogue.
16. Brian Hiatt, "Neil Gaiman on the Secret History of *The Sandman*, from Giant Mechanical Spiders to the Joker," *Rolling Stone*, August 23, 2022, https://www.rollingstone.com/tv-movies/tv-movie-features/neil-gaiman-sandman-season-2-release-good-omens-calliope-1234580270/.
17. Gaiman, *Annotated Sandman*, 22.19.4.
18. Gaiman, *Annotated Sandman*, 22.20.1.
19. Jahlmar, "Give the Devil His Due"; dela Cruz, "Narratives," 1–8; Porter, "Neil Gaiman's Lucifer."
20. Gaiman, *Annotated Sandman*, 23.1.2.
21. Dante, *Inferno* (trans. Cary), 3:95–96.

22. Gaiman, *Annotated Sandman*, 23.9.5.
23. Younus, "(Re)interpreting Dante's *Inferno*," 88.
24. Gaiman, *Annotated Sandman*, 22.23.1–2.
25. Gaiman, *Annotated Sandman*, 23.18.14.
26. Gaiman, *Annotated Sandman*, 23.15.3–4.
27. Gaiman, *Annotated Sandman*, 22.19.1.
28. Gaiman, *Annotated Sandman*, 28.22.5.
29. Porter, "Neil Gaiman's Lucifer," 181–82. The Midrash are extrascriptural interpretations and analyses of the Talmud. The Aggadic midrashim deal with nonlegal issues, including poetry, the afterlife, proverbs, and spirituality. "Gehenna" as both a word and a concept has a long and complicated history, but it has generally come to mean a place of punishment after death—but not eternal punishment. Judaism lacks a Hell as understood in Christian doctrine. Thanks to Leah Komar and Dani Raanan for discussions of Jewish theology.
30. Gaiman, *Annotated Sandman*, 23.10.3.
31. Gaiman, *Annotated Sandman*, 27.8.5–6.

Chapter Four | The Wizard Tim

1. Eichel, "Between Mimesis and Fantasy," 114–29.
2. The hero's journey is the narratological structure for mythology and fantasy made famous by Joseph Campbell in the late 1940s; see Campbell, *Hero with a Thousand Faces*. This parallel is noted by Roger Zelazny in his introduction to Gaiman's *The Books of Magic* (ii–iv); and Stephen Rauch performs an in-depth study of *Sandman* and the hero's journey in *Neil Gaiman's "The Sandman" and Joseph Campbell*. Other famous magical-apprenticeship stories include Ursula K. Le Guin, *A Wizard of Earthsea* (1968); J. K. Rowling, Harry Potter series (1997–2007); and T. H. White, *The Once and Future King* (1958). See Winslade, "Enrolling in the 'Hidden School.'"
3. Selling, "Fantastic Neomedievalism," 212.
4. Gaiman, *Books of Magic*, III.14.1.
5. Some academic argument exists over whether the *Commedia* can be considered a true dream vision.
6. Through Faerie, Tim accesses several other magical worlds of the DC Comics mythos: Skartaris (Warlord), Myrra (Showcase), Pytharia (Claw the Unconquered), Gemworld, and the Dreaming. He also gets a look at

Hell. Gaiman here reiterates his philosophy that people trap themselves out of guilt and expectation.

7. Gaiman, *Books of Magic*, III.33.4–5.
8. Eichel, "Between Mimesis and Fantasy," 120.
9. Murray, *Romance and Prophecies.*
10. Simpson, "King Arthur's Enchanted Sleep," 206.
11. Salisbury and Weldon, introduction to *Lybeaus Desconus.*
12. *Lybeaus Desconus*, lines 1353–460.
13. Gaiman, *Books of Magic*, III.39.1.
14. I've unpacked this further in a blog entry: Shiloh Carroll, "Sandman and the Faerie Tiend to Hell," November 5, 2020, https://shilohcarroll.wordpress.com/2020/11/05/sandman-faerie-tiend-to-hell/.
15. "I am sae fair and fu o flesh, / I'm feard it be mysel." "Tam Lin," stanza 24, in Child, *English and Scottish Popular Ballads.*
16. "Thomas Rhymer," stanza 57, in Child, *English and Scottish Popular Ballads.*
17. See Gaiman, *Annotated Sandman*, 2:139; Briggs, "English Fairies."
18. In the Vulgate cycle of Arthurian myth and continuing into Sir Thomas Malory's *Le Morte d'Arthur*, Merlin falls in love with Nimue, the Lady of the Lake, and teaches her magic, after which she imprisons him in a tower, an oak tree, or a cave.
19. Gaiman, *Books of Magic*, I.34.5.
20. Gaiman, *Books of Magic*, IV.34.4.
21. Gaiman, *Books of Magic*, IV.30.2.
22. Farley, *Cultural History of Tarot*, 95–96.
23. For a more detailed exploration of Romanticism and how it developed, see Chandler, *Dream of Order.*
24. Farley, *Cultural History of Tarot*, 129.
25. According to Gaiman's acknowledgments at the beginning of *The Books of Magic.*
26. Pollack, *Complete Illustrated Guide*, 42.
27. Gaiman, *Books of Magic*, III.2.3.

Chapter Five | "To the World"

1. Gaiman, "Neil Gaiman on Terry Pratchett," 405.
2. "Hard Times," *Good Omens*, season 1, episode 6, written by Neil Gaiman and directed by Doug Mackinnon.

3. Amanat, "Introduction," 2.
4. O'Hear and O'Hear, *Picturing the Apocalypse.*
5. O'Hear and O'Hear, *Picturing the Apocalypse,* 45; Hughes, *Constructing Antichrist,* 8–9.
6. Amanat, "Introduction," 4.
7. Amanat, "Introduction," 2–3; Court, *Approaching the Apocalypse,* 4–5.
8. He goes on like this for a bit. Wulfstan, "Sermo Lupi ad Anglos," 261.
9. Sheinfeld, "Scenes from the End of the World," 203–5.
10. Gaiman and Pratchett, *Good Omens,* 216.
11. Gaiman and Pratchett, *Good Omens,* 5.
12. Gaiman and Pratchett, *Good Omens,* 14.
13. Scott, "*And the World Continues to Spin,*" 80.
14. Gaiman and Pratchett, *Good Omens,* 224.
15. Scott, "*And the World Continues to Spin,*" 85.
16. Gaiman and Pratchett, *Good Omens,* 363.
17. Gaiman and Pratchett, *Good Omens,* 388.
18. "Saturday Morning Funtime," *Good Omens,* season 1, episode 4, written by Neil Gaiman and directed by Doug Mackinnon.
19. "The Very Last Day of the Rest of Their Lives," *Good Omens,* season 1, episode 6, written by Neil Gaiman and directed by Doug Mackinnon.
20. Scott, "*And the World Continues to Spin,*" 74.
21. Gaiman and Pratchett, *Good Omens,* 38.
22. Clemons, "Adapting Revelation," 89.
23. Gaiman and Pratchett, *Good Omens,* 30.
24. Luke Waters and Eleanor Janega discuss this trend, including a dog saint, in a Patreon-exclusive podcast episode: "Medieval Sainthood," *We're Not So Different,* March 10, 2022, https://www.patreon.com/posts/patreon-ep-63622618.
25. Gaiman and Pratchett, *Good Omens,* 24.
26. Unless otherwise noted, all discussion of women's hagiographies in this section are based on the stories as told by the medieval abbot Ælfric of Eynsham (c. 955–1010 CE) and translated and compiled by Donovan in *Women Saints' Lives.*
27. See Friesen, *Female Crucifix.*
28. Donovan, *Women Saints' Lives,* 121.
29. Gaiman and Pratchett, *Good Omens,* 24.

30. This isn't the only place in the novel that this dynamic is played for laughs; another Beryl appears late in the story as one of Madame Tracy's regular clients. She visits Tracy in order to keep the ghost of her dead husband, Ron, updated on her life and the family. For the most part, Madame Tracy is a benign fraud, but in this instance, Aziraphale happens to intervene while he's incorporeal and allows Ron through to speak to Beryl. He tells her (through a stutter) that she never let him speak while he was alive, and now that he's dead, he has one message for her: "Shut up" (Gaiman and Pratchett, *Good Omens*, 289). It raises the question of which author knew a talkative Beryl and needed to enshrine her.
31. Gaiman and Pratchett, *Good Omens*, 24.
32. Gaiman and Pratchett, *Good Omens*, 29–30.
33. Gaiman, introduction to *Quite Nice and Fairly Accurate Good Omens Script Book*, xi.
34. "Hard Times," *Good Omens*, season 1, episode 6.
35. Cunliffe, *Britain Begins*, 423.
36. Henshall, *Folly and Fortune*, 98–99; Higham and Ryan, *Anglo-Saxon World*, 235.
37. For an extensive overview of the King Arthur legend and its development, see Higham, *King Arthur.*
38. Thorpe, introduction to Geoffrey of Monmouth, *History of the Kings of Britain*, 9–10.
39. Per cinematographer Gavin Finney, quoted in Whyman, *Nice and Accurate*, 231. Thanks to Tumblr user Ixi, owner of the Fuck Yeah Good Omens Tumblr blog, for directing me to this passage.
40. Thanks to the wonderful denizens of the We're Not So Different podcast Discord server for helping me sort out and date the armor pieces.
41. Breiding, "Horse Armor."
42. Gavin Finney outright states that they were going for "part *Excalibur* and part *Monty Python*." Whyman, *Nice and Accurate*, 231.
43. This is, of course, ridiculous and untrue. Many medievalists and medievalismists have written about this; a representative example is Pugh and Weisl, *Medievalisms*.
44. Or Arthur is mortally wounded and taken away to Avalon, depending on who's doing the telling. Higham, *King Arthur*, 95.

Chapter Six | Poisoned Apples and Magic Roses

1. Tolkien, "On Fairy-Stories," 120–21.
2. Attebery, *Strategies of Fantasy*, 11–12.
3. Gaiman, introduction to *Fragile Things*, xxiv.
4. Warner, *From the Beast to the Blonde.*
5. Hoogenboezem, "Medievalism and Magic," 249–50, 268–69.
6. They were also trying to create a medieval heritage for Germany for nationalist reasons. Ziolkowski, *Fairy Tales from Before Fairy Tales*, 23–24.
7. Pugh, "Introduction," 5.
8. Ziolkowski, *Fairy Tales from Before Fairy Tales*, 23; Hoogenboezem, "Medievalism and Magic," 255.
9. Bradford, "Where Happily Ever After," 175.
10. Warner, *From the Beast to the Blonde*, 207.
11. Sturtevant, "You Don't Learn It Deliberately," 80.
12. Bradford, "Where Happily Ever After," 178.
13. Respectively, Disney films *Beauty and the Beast* (1991), *Sleeping Beauty* (1959), and *Aladdin* (1992).
14. Jade Lum, "Un-training the Imagination," 51.
15. Warner, *From the Beast to the Blonde*, 417.
16. Gaiman, "Some Reflections," 60–62.
17. Gaiman, "Some Reflections," 54.
18. Gaiman, "Once Upon a Time."
19. Gaiman, "Some Reflections," 59.
20. Drury, "Gaiman," 110.
21. Gutierrez, "Weaving New Dreams," 217–18.
22. Gaiman, "Snow, Glass, Apples," 334.
23. Gaiman, "Snow, Glass, Apples," 345.
24. Gaiman, "Snow, Glass, Apples," 331; Law, "Fairest of All," 182.
25. Law, "Fairest of All," 188.
26. Law, "Fairest of All," 181.
27. Law, "Fairest of All," 183–84.
28. Warner, *From the Beast to the Blonde*, 227.
29. Ussher, *Managing the Monstrous Feminine*, 3.
30. Law, "Fairest of All," 178.
31. Ussher, *Managing the Monstrous Feminine*, 21.
32. Klapcsik, "Neil Gaiman's Irony," 326–27.

33. Gaiman, "Snow, Glass, Apples," 345.
34. Drury, "Gaiman," 114–15.
35. Gaiman, *Sleeper and the Spindle*, 14.
36. D. Russell, "Damsels in Deep Rest No More," 179.
37. Gutierrez, "Weaving New Dreams," 224–25.
38. Lum, "Un-training the Imagination," 49.
39. On the exceptional woman in medievalist fantasy, see Tolmie, "Medievalism and the Fantasy Heroine"; Barr, *Alien to Femininity*, 85.
40. Gaiman, *Sleeper and the Spindle*, 35.
41. Warner, *From the Beast to the Blonde*, 412.
42. Gaiman, *Sleeper and the Spindle*, 59.
43. Gaiman, *Sleeper and the Spindle*, 16.
44. Gaiman, *Sleeper and the Spindle*, 49.
45. Lum, "Un-training the Imagination," 47.
46. Lum, "Un-training the Imagination," 47–48.
47. Warner, *From the Beast to the Blonde*, 24.
48. Gaiman, *The Sleeper and the Spindle*, 66.

Chapter Seven | "Go and Catch a Falling Star"

1. Only *Good Omens* (1990), coauthored with Terry Pratchett, and *Neverwhere* (1996), the novelization of Gaiman's scripts for the BBC miniseries, predate *Stardust* for pure prose releases.
2. Neil Gaiman, reply to Tumblr Ask, October 22, 2020, https://neil-gaiman.tumblr.com/post/632722291994804224/hi-mr-gaiman-i-recently-started-reading-stardust.
3. Wolfe, "Neil Gaiman," 372.
4. Ashton, *Medieval English Romance*, 14–15.
5. Barron, *English Medieval Romance*, 8.
6. Rider, "Other Worlds of Romance," 120.
7. Ashton, *Medieval English Romance*, 51, 94.
8. P. Brown, "*Stardust* as Allegorical *Bildungsroman*," 220, 224.
9. Most notably the *Prose Tristram*; and Sir Thomas Malory's "The Book of Sir Tristram de Lyones," in *Le Morte Darthur*.
10. Knight, "Social Function," 104.
11. Knight, "Social Function," 104.
12. Hardiman, *Matter of Identity*, 2.

13. Gaiman, *Stardust*, 1.
14. Collected in Marie de France, *Lays*.
15. Wade, *Fairies in Medieval Romance*, 112; Briggs, *Fairies in Tradition and Literature*, 60.
16. Maddox and Sturm-Maddox, introduction to d'Arras, *Melusine*, 2.
17. Byrne, "Fairy Lovers," 99-100.
18. P. Brown, "*Stardust* as Allegorical *Bildungsroman*," 228.
19. Thanks in particular to Leah Komar for extensive discussions on Jewish mythology and Hebrew etymology.
20. Gaiman, *Stardust*, 106.
21. One critic argues that using "childish" rhymes with actual power is another, more subtle way that Gaiman pushes back against Donne's poem. P. Brown, "*Stardust* as Allegorical *Bildungsroman*," 225.
22. Mendelesohn and James, *Short History of Fantasy*, 13, 17.
23. Gaiman, *Stardust*, 2.
24. Gaiman, *Stardust*, 5.
25. Collins, "Fairy and Faerie."
26. Gaiman, *Stardust*, 5.
27. Zipes, *Victorian Fairy Tales*, xii–xiv.
28. Hutton, "Making Of," 1148.
29. Zipes, *Victorian Fairy Tales*, xvi, xx–xxiii.
30. Zipes, *Victorian Fairy Tales*, xxix.
31. Keightley, *Fairy Mythology*, 13.
32. John Black, *The Falls of Clyde, or The Fairies* (1806), 13, https://archive.org/details/fallsclydeorfai00blagoog/page/n10/mode/2up.
33. N. Brown, *Fairies*, 163.
34. Gaiman, *Stardust*, 10, 13.
35. Gaiman, *Stardust*, 54.
36. Gaiman, *Stardust*, 63.
37. P. Brown, "*Stardust* as Allegorical *Bildungsroman*," 220.
38. Gaiman, *Stardust*, 63–64.
39. Zipes, *Victorian Fairy Tales*, xxv.
40. Zipes, *Victorian Fairy Tales*, xxv–xxvi.
41. Gaiman, *Stardust*, 279.
42. Donne, "Song," line 18, in *Poems*.
43. Bloom, *John Donne*, 18.

44. P. Brown, "*Stardust* as Allegorical *Bildungsroman*," 216.
45. P. Brown, "*Stardust* as Allegorical *Bildungsroman*," 218.
46. Crofts and Hatter, in "Fairy Tale That Won't Behave," 34–35, note that money, youth, and beauty are consistently linked throughout the novel—for example, Una's suggestion to Dunstan that the snowdrop might cost gray hair.
47. Cahill, "Through the Looking Glass," 61.
48. Creed, *Monstrous Feminine*, 83.
49. See Kristeva, *Powers of Horror*.
50. Gaiman, *Stardust*, 323.
51. Crofts and Hatter, "Fairy Tale That Won't Behave," 22–23.
52. Crofts and Hatter, "Fairy Tale That Won't Behave," 31.
53. Crofts and Hatter, in "Fairy Tale That Won't Behave," 25, note that Una isn't included in the naming system of her brothers but starts a new list. The brothers are all considered equally potential heirs; Una is not.
54. Curry, "Pale Trees Shook," 21–22.
55. Gaiman, *Stardust*, 130.
56. Gaiman, *Stardust*, 138.
57. Gaiman, *Stardust*, 185.
58. Gaiman, *Stardust*, 186.
59. Curry, "Pale Trees Shook," 31.
60. In *Stardust*, writers Matthew Vaughn and Jane Goldman name the witches rather than using the collective term Lilim: Lamia (played by Michelle Pfeiffer), Empusa (Sarah Alexander), and Mormo (Joanna Scanlan). All three are Greek demons known for deceiving men and devouring children; see Purkiss, *At the Bottom of the Garden*. I don't have space here to address the interesting shift from Hebrew to Greek naming choices.
61. Cahill, "Through the Looking Glass," 65.
62. Crofts and Hatter, "Fairy Tale That Won't Behave," 37–38.
63. "A Magical Fairy Tale Hits the Big Screen," *Talk of the Nation*, August 8, 2007, https://www.npr.org/templates/story/story.php?storyId=12594675.

Chapter Eight | "Loki Has Done This"

1. Hume, "Loki and Odin," 298.
2. Larrington, introduction to *Poetic Edda*, xi–xii.

3. The manuscript is called AM 748; the AM refers to the Arnamagnæn Collection in Copenhagen, where it was located until being transferred to Iceland in the late twentieth century. Lindow, *Norse Mythology*, 14.
4. You won't find the *Háttatal* in most translated versions of the *Prose Edda* simply because it's long, technical, and obscure. Byock, introduction to Snorri, *Prose Edda*, xiv–xvii.
5. Byock, introduction to Snorri, *Prose Edda*, xiv.
6. Snorri, *Prose Edda*, 1–8
7. Lindow, *Norse Mythology*, 22.
8. Geoffrey of Monmouth, *History of the Kings of Britain*, 54–74.
9. Machan, "Snorri's *Edda*," 304.
10. Machan, "Snorri's *Edda*," 305.
11. Larrington, introduction to *Poetic Edda*, xiii.
12. Byock, introduction to Snorri, *Prose Edda*, xvii.
13. Lindow, *Norse Mythology*, 34–36.
14. Larrington, introduction to *Poetic Edda*, xxi–xxii; Machan, "Snorri's *Edda*," 296–97.
15. Machan, "Snorri's *Edda*," 298–99.
16. Larrington, introduction to *Poetic Edda*, xxii.
17. Larrington, introduction to *Poetic Edda*, xxiii.
18. Kaufman and Sturtevant, *Devil's Historians*, 55–58.
19. See Dorothy Kim, "White Supremacists Have Weaponized an Imaginary Viking Past. It's Time to Reclaim the Real History," *Time*, April 15, 2019, https://time.com/5569399/viking-history-white-nationalists/; Natalie Van Deusen, "Why Teaching about the Viking Age Is Relevant—And Even Crucial," Canadian Historical Association, November 25, 2019, https://cha-shc.ca/teaching/teachers-blog/why-teaching-about-the-viking-age-is-relevant-and-even-crucial-2019-11-25.htm; Lavin, *Culture Warlords*.
20. Gaiman, *Norse Mythology*, 11–12; Gaiman, "Some Reflections," 54.
21. Lyall, "Neil Gaiman on His *Norse Mythology*."
22. Gaiman in Sommers, *Conversations with Neil Gaiman*, 201.
23. Lyall, "Neil Gaiman on His *Norse Mythology*."
24. Lisa L. Hannett, "The Politics of Retelling *Norse Mythology*," *Atlantic*, February 23, 2017, https://www.theatlantic.com/entertainment/archive/2017/02/the-politics-of-retelling-norse-mythology/517422/; Neil Gaiman, "*Norse Mythology* Release Date Announcement," Facebook, September 14,

2016, https://www.facebook.com/300224781015/photos/a.306989681015/10153810442141016/.

25. Hannett, "Politics."
26. Gaiman, "Some Reflections," 59–61.
27. "Neil Gaiman: 'I Like Being British. Even When I'm Ashamed, I'm Fascinated,'" interview with Michelle Dean, *Guardian*, February 4, 2017, https://www.theguardian.com/books/2017/feb/04/neil-gaiman-interview-books.
28. Larrington, "Our Return to Twilight."
29. Larrington, introduction to *Poetic Edda*, xiii.
30. Bartle, "Betwixt the Eddas," 246.
31. Gaiman, *Norse Mythology*, 21.
32. Bartle, "Betwixt the Eddas," 247.
33. For example, Gaiman tells us that Odin traded an eye for wisdom (*Völuspá* verse 28, *Gylfaginning* section 15); that he hanged himself from Yggdrasil to gain wisdom and magic (*Havamal* verses 138–42); that he has dozens of names (*Grimnismal* verses 46–50, *Völuspá* throughout, and *Gylfaginning* section 3 and section 20); and that he has a pair of ravens named Huginn and Muninn (*Grimnismal* verse 20 and *Gylfaginning* section 38). Citations from the *Poetic Edda* are listed by poem and verse, and those from Snorri's *Prose Edda* by numbered section.
34. Snorri, *Prose Edda*, *Gylfaginning* section 20.
35. The *Ynglinga Saga* is not included in the Eddas, but it is included in Snorri's *Heimskringla*, a collection of Norse sagas and histories of Norwegian and Swedish kings.
36. Gaiman, *Norse Mythology*, 46–47.
37. Gaiman, *Norse Mythology*, 15.
38. Gaiman, *Norse Mythology*, 29–30.
39. Gaiman's spelling of "Gjallarhorn."
40. Gaiman's spelling of "Jormungandr."
41. Snorri, *Prose Edda*, *Gylfaginning* section 38.
42. Gaiman, *Norse Mythology*, 24.
43. Wanner, "Cunning Intelligence," 229.
44. Gaiman doesn't relate this story in *Norse Mythology*, probably because it's mentioned only briefly in Snorri's *Prose Edda*.
45. Snorri, *Prose Edda*, *Gylfaginning* section 53. Though Snorri cites *Prose Edda*,

Völuspá section 39, here, those lines in context do not seem to refer to a post-Ragnarök era but rather are part of the badness that happens just before Ragnarök.

46. Gaiman, *Norse Mythology*, 283.
47. Much of this playing down is accomplished simply by skipping over the actual text of the *Lokasenna* (Loki's quarrel) from the *Poetic Edda*, in which Loki airs everyone's dirty laundry.
48. There are no surviving stories that explain this further.
49. *Thrymskvida*, in *Poetic Edda*, verse 13.
50. Larrington, introduction to *Poetic Edda*, 97.
51. *Lokasenna*, in *Poetic Edda*, verses 30–32.
52. Gaiman, *Norse Mythology*, 114.
53. Neil Gaiman, response to Tumblr Ask, January 12, 2022, https://neil-gaiman.tumblr.com/post/673232678437404672/my-norse-mythology-lecturer-loves-your-work-but.

Chapter Nine | Odin and Low Key and Shadow

1. Gaiman, "How Dare You," 65.
2. Gaiman in Sommers, *Conversations with Neil Gaiman*, 110.
3. Gaiman, *American Gods*, 62–64.
4. Joiner, "Valhalla Anew!," 129.
5. Gaiman, "Brief Lives: Chapter 8," *Sandman* 48 (1993): 16.1, in *Annotated Sandman*, 3:269–94.
6. See Braucher and Orbach, "Scamming."
7. Gaiman, *American Gods*, 83.
8. Gaiman, *American Gods*, 472.
9. Gaiman, *American Gods*, 482.
10. Gaiman, *American Gods*, 511.
11. Gaiman, *American Gods*, 517.
12. *Völuspá*, in *Poetic Edda* section 59.
13. Joiner, "Valhalla Anew!," 141.
14. Gaiman, *American Gods*, 369.
15. Gaiman, *American Gods*, 425.
16. Gaiman, *American Gods*, 171.
17. Gaiman, *American Gods*, 95; editor Klinger notes that Wednesday is paraphrasing a quote commonly attributed to Louis-Antoine Saint-Just, one

of the principal architects of the Reign of Terror (in Gaiman, *Annotated American Gods*, 121).

18. Blomqvist, "Road," 10–12, 16.
19. Gaiman, *Annotated American Gods*, 251. He notes that it comes from a Northumbrian fairy tale about a child outwitting a fairy.
20. Gorman, "Neil Gaiman's *American Gods*," 177–78.
21. Sodeman, "*American Gods* and Where to Find Them," 70.
22. Gaiman, *American Gods*, 85.
23. Gaiman in Sommers, *Conversations with Neil Gaiman*, 92.
24. Blomqvist, "Road," 23.
25. Gaiman, *American Gods*, 348.
26. Gaiman, *American Gods*, 477.
27. Bossert, "To Survive," 44.
28. Carroll, "Imagined Nation," 309–10.
29. Gaiman, *American Gods*, 123.
30. Carroll, "Imagined Nation," 318.
31. See, e.g., MacColl, "King Arthur and the Making of an English Britain."
32. Gorman, "Neil Gaiman's *American Gods*," 170.
33. Gorman, "Neil Gaiman's *American Gods*," 171.

Chapter Ten | "Eating, Drinking, Killing, and Fornicating"

1. As with all films, Zemeckis's *Beowulf* was a team effort, written by Roger Avary and Neil Gaiman, directed by Robert Zemeckis, and starring Ray Winstone, Anthony Hopkins, Crispin Glover, and Robin Wright. Decisions made regarding the adaptation were also largely a team effort. Several choices are attributed specifically to Gaiman in the metatextual material (*Beowulf, the Script Book*, behind-the-scenes DVD featurettes, etc.), and Gaiman's usual thematic material is clear, but unlike Gaiman's novels, little of the final product can truly be attributed to him.
2. The document is known as Cotton Vitellius A.xv, for the library (Sir Robert Cotton's), the shelf on which Cotton kept it (under a bust of Aulus Vitellius, emperor of Rome in the first century CE), and the position on that shelf (the fifteenth book on the top shelf). The manuscript was damaged in 1731 CE when the library that housed it at Ashburnham House caught fire, then was neglected, creating more damage as the manuscript crumbled.

3. Jones, "From Heorot to Hollywood," 13.
4. Liuzza, introduction to *Beowulf*, 12.
5. Tolkien, "Monsters," 5–48.
6. Medievalists are notoriously slow to adopt critical theories and quick to dismiss them as fads, as Finke and Shichtman note in *Medieval Texts and Contemporary Readers* (3–4).
7. Risden, "Cinematic Commoditization," 67.
8. Bildhauer, *Filming the Middle Ages*, 19.
9. Bernau, "Suspended Animation."
10. Bildhauer, *Filming the Middle Ages*, 20.
11. Baudrillard, *Simulacra and Simulation*.
12. See, e.g., Hodapp, "Arthur, Beowulf."
13. *King Arthur*, written by David Franzoni, directed by Antoine Fuqua (Touchstone, 2004).
14. Kershaw and Ormond, "We Are the Monsters Now."
15. *Beowulf, the Script Book*, 5.
16. His doubts about the fight against Grendel's mother may be based on a misreading of the text. One critic breaks down the Old English and its translations to show that where Avary and Gaiman think Beowulf was fighting Grendel's mother for eight days, it was probably eight hours. Jones, in "From Heorot to Hollywood," 24–25.
17. *Beowulf, the Script Book*, 10.
18. Zemeckis in "Origins of *Beowulf*," a DVD special feature.
19. Zemeckis in "Origins of *Beowulf*." He dates it to "between the seventh and twelfth centuries" and claims it's "the first thing ever written in the English language."
20. "Hero's Journey," *Beowulf* DVD special feature.
21. Kershaw and Ormond, "We Are the Monsters Now."
22. Niles, "Introduction," 4.
23. Robinson, "Beowulf," 142–43, 148–52.
24. Haydock and Risden, *"Beowulf" on Film*, 88–89.
25. While in the poem Beowulf does accuse Unferth of kinslaying and imply that he is emblematic of the weakness of Hrothgar's court that leads to Grendel's attacks (lines 587–601), the statement in the film that Unferth killed his brothers because he caught them having sex with their mother is unique to the film.
26. Forni, "Popularizing High Culture," 51.

27. Roman, "Use of Nature," 56.
28. Haydock and Risden, *"Beowulf" on Film*, 114.
29. "Exclusive Interview: Neil Gaiman (*Beowulf*)," conducted by David Faraci, CHUD.com, November 9, 2007, https://chud.com/12435/exclusive-interview-neil-gaiman-beowulf/.
30. For example, Liuzza's translation of *Beowulf* renders *æglæca* variously as "great ravager" (line 159), "evil beast" (433), "monster" (556, 732), and "great creatures" (2592).
31. A lack of lineage for Grendel is part of the point; in early English culture, "a man's pedigree is an important marker of identity," so Grendel's having none makes him an outsider and an enigma. Hodapp, "*No hie fæder cunnon*," 101.
32. Kershaw and Ormond, "We Are the Monsters Now."
33. Risden, "Cinematic Commoditization," 79.
34. Risden, "The Hero, the Mad Male Id," 119–20, 130.
35. Forni, "Popularizing High Culture," 51; Haydock and Risden, *"Beowulf" on Film*, 162.
36. Osmond, review of *Beowulf*, 61; Ebert, "*Beowulf*."
37. Risden, "The Hero, the Mad Male Id," 120.
38. Haydock and Risden, *"Beowulf" on Film*, 28–30.
39. Risden, "Cinematic Commoditization," 67.
40. Jones, "From Heorot to Hollywood," 19.
41. Qtd. in Forni, "Popularizing High Culture," 45.
42. "What We Do," Young Minds Inspired, n.d., http://youngmindsinspired.com/what-we-do.
43. "*Beowulf*," Young Minds Inspired, 2007, https://ymiclassroom.com/wp-content/uploads/2012/03/Beowulf.pdf.
44. Jones, "From Heorot to Hollywood," 23.
45. Haydock and Risden, *"Beowulf" on Film*, 65.

Chapter Eleven | Where Shadow Meets Grendel

1. Gaiman, introduction to *Smoke and Mirrors*, 26.
2. The earlier story was "Only the End of the World Again," written for *Shadows over Innsmouth* in 1994 and collected in *Smoke and Mirrors* in 1998.
3. Gaiman, introduction to *Fragile Things*, xxxii; Gaiman, introduction to *Trigger Warning*, xxxvi.

4. Lionarons, "*Beowulf*," 2.
5. Liuzza, introduction to *Beowulf*, 14.
6. Fulk, Bjork, and Niles, introduction to *Klaeber's "Beowulf,"* xxxvi.
7. Kershaw and Ormond, "We Are the Monsters Now."
8. Baz Luhrmann's *William Shakespeare's Romeo + Juliet* came out in 1996, just a couple of years before Gaiman wrote "Bay Wolf." It also features a fictional California beach city (Verona Beach), lots of drugs, and beautiful, surgically enhanced young people.
9. Gaiman, "Monarch," 326.
10. Gaiman, "Monarch," 331.
11. And bare bodied; the rich people strip him naked first. The poem's Beowulf fights armorless, but not fully naked.
12. Gaiman, "Bay Wolf," lines 45–47.
13. Gaiman, "Monarch," 284.
14. Cohen, "Monster Culture," 46.
15. Forni, *Beowulf's Popular Afterlife*, 15; Asma, *On Monsters*, 10; Graham, *Representations*, 40.
16. Immediately after Heorot is built, the poet foreshadows its destruction: "The time was not yet at hand / when the sword-hate of sworn in-laws / should arise after ruthless violence" (*Beowulf* [trans. Liuzza], lines 83–85). During the celebration held after Grendel's defeat, the poet notes that the people are united; they were not plotting "false treacheries [. . .] at that time," suggesting that plots would come later (1018–19). A bit later, the poet hints again that "their peace was still whole then / each true to the other," again implying that it won't always be so (1164–65).
17. Lionarons, "*Beowulf*," 11–12.
18. Gaiman, "Bay Wolf," lines 22, 37.
19. Gaiman, "Bay Wolf," lines 135–37.
20. Interestingly, "Only the End of the World Again" shares many plot beats and themes as "Bay Wolf" and "The Monarch of the Glen": Talbot finds himself in Innsmouth, where the servants of the Deep Ones are attempting to raise the gods. He fights Madame Ezekiel, an avatar of one of the Deep Ones, in an underwater citadel in a struggle that contains erotic overtones. He prevents, or at least postpones, the end of the world, standing between humanity and the existential threat of the Old Gods.
21. Jennie explains *hulders* and their propensity to fall in love with and marry human men to Shadow. Gaiman, *American Gods*, 296–97.

22. Gaiman, "Monarch," 326.
23. Gaiman, "Monarch," 294, 322.
24. Forni, *Beowulf's Popular Afterlife*, 144–45.
25. Gaiman, "Bay Wolf," line 17.
26. Gaiman, "Bay Wolf," line 186.
27. Forni, *Beowulf's Popular Afterlife*, 151.
28. Forni, *Beowulf's Popular Afterlife*, 150.
29. Gaiman, "Monarch," 291–92.
30. Gaiman, "Monarch," 333.
31. Gaiman, "Monarch," 337.
32. Gaiman, "Keepsakes and Treasures," 112.
33. Forni, *Beowulf's Popular Afterlife*, 150.
34. Gaiman, "Bay Wolf," lines 1 and 8.
35. Liuzza's translation of *Beowulf* renders it as "Listen"; Seamus Heaney as "So"; Tolkien as "Lo"; and Maria Dahvana Headley as "Bro!" There's been a not insignificant amount of debate over the translation and grammatical status of the word; see Walkden, "Status of *hwæt* in Old English."
36. The Beowulf poet prefers understatement and irony to outright humor, though wordplay does appear in the poem. Risden, "Heroic Humor in *Beowulf*," 77.
37. Gaiman, "Bay Wolf," line 14.
38. Gaiman, "Bay Wolf," line 126.
39. *Beowulf* (ed. Liuzza), line 991, my translation.
40. *Beowulf* (ed. Liuzza), line 1545, my translation.
41. For more on appositives in *Beowulf*, see Robinson, *Beowulf and the Appositive Style*.
42. *Beowulf* (trans. Liuzza), lines 1273–76.
43. *Beowulf* (trans. Liuzza), lines 29–30 and 50.
44. Gaiman, "Bay Wolf," lines 185–88.

Epilogue | "Make Good Art"

1. Schweitzer, "Tapdancing," 116.
2. Gaiman, *Odd and the Frost Giants* (2008). This text is also available in an edition illustrated by Chris Riddell; see Gaiman, *Odd and the Frost Giants* (2016).
3. Gaiman, "Chivalry" ([1993] 2007).

4. Colleen Doran, "Neil Gaiman's *Chivalry*: From Illuminated Manuscripts to Comics," January 28, 2023, https://www.tumblr.com/colleendoran/707713432833687553/neil-gaimans-chivalry-from-illuminated.
5. Behold the vast field of academic articles and books on George R. R. Martin's Song of Ice and Fire series, to which I have contributed a not insignificant amount. I am just as guilty of the "that's not really medieval, but whatever" approach as anyone else.
6. Every time a politician says something is "medieval" or is "sending us back to the Dark Ages," a medievalismist gets her wings.
7. Such as white supremacist appropriation of Viking culture and symbolism.
8. Gaiman, "Make Good Art," 456.

REFERENCES

Aladdin. Written by Ron Clements, John Musker, Ted Elliot, and Terry Rossio. Directed by Ron Clements and John Musker. Walt Disney Productions, 1992.

Albin, Andrew, Mary C. Erler, Thomas O'Donnell, et al., eds. *Whose Middle Ages? Teachable Moments for an Ill-Used Past*. New York: Fordham University Press, 2019.

Amanat, Abbas. "Introduction: Apocalyptic Anxieties and Millennial Hopes in the Salvation Religions of the Middle East." In *Imagining the End: Visions of Apocalypse from the Ancient Middle East to Modern America*, edited by Abbas Amanat and Magnus T. Bernhardsson, 1–19. London: I. B. Tauris, 2002.

Ashley, Kathleen. "Titivillus and the Battle of Words in *Mankind*." *Annuale Mediaevale* 16 (1975): 128–50.

Ashton, Gail. *Medieval English Romance in Context*. London: Continuum, 2010.

Asma, Stephen T. *On Monsters: An Unnatural History of Our Worst Fears*. Oxford: Oxford University Press, 2009.

Attebery, Brian. *Strategies of Fantasy*. Bloomington: Indiana University Press, 1992.

Barr, Marleen S. *Alien to Femininity: Speculative Fiction and Feminist Theory*. New York: Greenwood, 1987.

Barron, W. R. J. *English Medieval Romance*. New York: Longman, 1987.

Bartle, Kimberlee. "Betwixt the Eddas: Situating Neil Gaiman's *Norse Mythology*." *Fantastika Journal* 1, no. 2 (2017): 246–48.

Baudrillard, Jean. *Simulacra and Simulation*. Translated by Sheila Faria Glaser. Ann Arbor: University of Michigan Press, 1981.

Beauty and the Beast. Written by Linda Woolverton. Directed by Gary Trousdale and Kirk Wise. Walt Disney Productions, 1991.

Beowulf. Introduced and translated by R. M. Liuzza. 2nd ed. Broadview, 2013.

Beowulf. Written by Mark Leahy and David Chappe. Directed by Graham Baker. Threshold, 1999.

Beowulf. Written by Roger Avary and Neil Gaiman. Directed by Robert Zemeckis. Image Movers and Shangri-La Entertainment, 2007.

Beowulf and Grendel. Written by Andrew Rai Berzins. Directed by Sturla Gunnarsson. Truly Indie, 2006.

Beowulf, the Script Book: As Told by Neil Gaiman and Roger Avary. New York: HarperCollins, 2007.

Bernau, Anke. "Suspended Animation: Myth, Memory, and History in *Beowulf*." *Screening the Past* 26 (2009). http://www.screeningthepast.com/issue-26-special-issue-early-europe/suspended-animation-myth-memory-and-history-in%c2%a0beowulf/.

Bildhauer, Bettina. *Filming the Middle Ages*. London: Reaktion, 2011.

Blomqvist, Rut. "The Road of Our Senses: Search for Personal Meaning and the Limitations of Myth in Neil Gaiman's *American Gods*." *Mythlore* 30, no. 3/4 (2012): 5–26.

Bloom, Harold. *John Donne: Comprehensive Research and Study Guide*. Chelsea House, 1999.

Bocharova, Jean. "Personification Allegory and Embodied Cognition." In *Personification: Embodying Meaning and Emotion*, edited by Walter S. Melion and Bart Ramakers, 43–69. Leiden: Brill, 2016.

Boethius. *The Consolation of Philosophy*. Translated by V. E. Watts. London: Penguin, 1969.

Bossert, Ray. "To Survive, You Must Believe." In *Neil Gaiman and Philosophy: Gods Gone Wild!*, edited by Tracy L. Bealer, Rachel Luria, and Wayne Yuen, 37–48. Open Court, 2012.

Bradford, Clare. "'Where Happily Ever After Happens Every Day': The Medievalisms of Disney's Princesses." In Pugh and Aronstein, *Disney Middle Ages*, 171–88.

Braucher, Jean, and Barak Orbach. "Scamming: The Misunderstood Confidence Man." *Yale Journal of Law and the Humanities* 27, no. 2 (2015): 249–90.

Breiding, Dirk. "Horse Armor in Medieval and Renaissance Europe: An Overview." In *The Armored Horse in Europe, 1480–1620*, edited by Stuart W. Phyrr, Donald J. LaRocca, and Dirk H. Breiding, 8–18. New Haven, CT: Yale University Press, 2005.

Briggs, Katharine. "The English Fairies." *Folklore* 68, no. 1 (1957): 270–87.

Briggs, Katharine. *The Fairies in Tradition and Literature*. New York: Routledge, 1967.

Brown, Nicola. *Fairies in Nineteenth-Century Art and Literature*. Cambridge: Cambridge University Press, 2001.

Brown, Paula. "*Stardust* as Allegorical *Bildungsroman*: An Apology for Platonic Idealism." *Extrapolation* 51, no. 2 (2010): 216–34.

Byock, Jesse L. Introduction to *The Prose Edda*, by Snorri Sturluson, ix–xxx. London: Penguin, 2005.

Byrne, Aisling. "Fairy Lovers: Sexuality, Order and Narrative in Medieval Romance." In *Sexual Culture in the Literature of Medieval Britain*, edited by Amanda Hopkins, Robert Allen Rouse, and Cory James Rushton, 99–110. Woodbridge, UK: Boydell & Brewer, 2014.

Cahill, Susan. "Through the Looking Glass: Fairy-Tale Cinema and the Spectacle of Femininity in *Stardust* and *The Brothers Grimm*." *Marvels and Tales* 24, no. 1 (2010): 57–67.

Campbell, Joseph. *The Hero with a Thousand Faces*. 3rd ed. Princeton, NJ: Princeton University Press, 1949.

Carroll, Siobhan. "Imagined Nation: Place and National Identity in Neil Gaiman's *American Gods*." *Extrapolation* 53, no. 3 (2012): 307–26.

The Castle of Perseverance. Edited by David N. Klausner. University of Rochester, 2010. https://d.lib.rochester.edu/teams/text/klausner-castle-of-perseverance. Accessed February 8, 2023.

Chandler, Alice. *A Dream of Order: The Medieval Ideal in Nineteenth-Century English Literature*. Lincoln: University of Nebraska Press, 1970.

Chaucer, Geoffrey. *The Complete Poetry and Prose of Geoffrey Chaucer*. 2nd ed. Edited by John H. Fisher. Thompson, 1989.

Child, Francis James. *The English and Scottish Popular Ballads*. Vol. 1. Dover, 1965. https://www.gutenberg.org/files/44969/44969-h/44969-h.htm.

Clemons, Amy Lea. "Adapting Revelation: *Good Omens* as Comic Corrective." *Journal of the Fantastic in the Arts* 28, no. 1 (2017): 86–101.

Cohen, Jeffrey Jerome. "Monster Culture (Seven Theses)." In *Classic Readings on Monster Theory*, edited by Asa Simon Mittman and Marcus Hensel, 44–54. Arc Humanities Press, 2018.

Collins, Meredith. "Fairy and Faerie: Uses of the Victorian in Neil Gaiman's and Charles Vess's *Stardust*." *ImageText* 4, no. 1 (2008). https://imagetextjournal.com/fairy-and-faerie-uses-of-the-victorian-in-neil-gaimans-and-charles-vesss-stardust/.

Court, John M. *Approaching the Apocalypse: A Short History of Christian Millenarianism*. London: I. B. Tauris, 2008.

Creed, Barbara. *The Monstrous Feminine*. New York: Routledge, 1993.

Crofts, Matthew, and Janine Hatter. "'The Fairy Tale that Won't Behave'? Ageing and Gender in Neil Gaiman's *Stardust* and Matthew Vaughn's Film Adaptation." *Femspec* 16, no. 1 (2015): 19–43.

Cunliffe, Barry. *Britain Begins*. Oxford: Oxford University Press, 2013.

Curry, Alice. "'The Pale Trees Shook, Although No Wind Blew, and It Seemed to Tristran that They Shook in Anger': 'Blind Space' and Ecofeminism in a Post-colonial Reading of Neil Gaiman and Charles Vess' Graphic Novel *Stardust* (1998)." *Barnboken* 33, no. 2 (2010): 19–33. https://barnboken.net/index.php/clr/article/view/16/16.

Dante Alighieri. *The Divine Comedy*. Translated by H. F. Cary. London: Cassell, 1892. https://www.gutenberg.org/files/8800/8800-h/8800-h.htm.

Dante Alighieri. *Inferno*. Translated by H. F. Cary. Chicago: Charles C. Thompson, 1814. https://babel.hathitrust.org/cgi/pt?id=uiug.30112001610424.

Dante Alighieri. *Inferno*. Translated by Michael Palma. Edited by Guiseppe Mazzotta. New York: Norton, 2008.

dela Cruz, Noelle Leslie. "Narratives of Suffering and Forgiveness: Neil Gaiman's *Seasons of Mists* as a Parable of Hell." In *Webbing Vicissitudes of Forgiveness*, edited by Karen Bettez Halnon, 1–8. Leiden: Brill, 2019.

Donne, John. *Poems*. John Marriot, 1633. https://www.bl.uk/collection-items/first-edition-of-john-donnes-poems-1633.

Donovan, Leslie A. *Women Saints' Lives in Old English Prose*. Woodbridge, UK: D. S. Brewer, 1999.

Drury, Leslie. "Gaiman: The Teller of Tales and the Fairy Tale Tradition." In *The Mythological Dimensions of Neil Gaiman*, edited by Anthony Burdge, Jessica Burke, and Kristine Larsen, 109–24. Kitsune, 2012.

Ebert, Roger. "*Beowulf*: I Am the Very Model of a Medieval Monster Slaughterer." RogerEbert.com, November 14, 2007. https://www.rogerebert.com/reviews/beowulf-2007.

Eichel, Andrew. "Between Mimesis and Fantasy: Binaries and Boundaries in *The Books of Magic*." In Sommers and Eveleth, *Artistry of Neil Gaiman*, 114–29.

Farley, Helen. *A Cultural History of Tarot: From Entertainment to Esotericism*. London: I. B. Tauris, 2009.

Faxton, Alicia. "The Pre-Raphaelite Brotherhood as Knights of the Round Table." In *Pre-Raphaelitism and Medievalism in the Arts*, edited by Liana De Girolami Cheney, 53–74. Lewiston, NY: Edwin Mellen, 1992.

Finke, Laurie A., and Martin B. Shichtman. "Introduction: Critical Theory and the Study of the Middle Ages." In *Medieval Texts and Contemporary Readers*, edited by Laurie A. Finke and Martin B. Shichtman, 1–12. Ithaca, NY: Cornell University Press, 1987.

Forni, Kathleen. *Beowulf's Popular Afterlife in Literature, Comic Books, and Film*. New York: Routledge, 2018.

Forni, Kathleen. "Popularizing High Culture: Zemeckis's *Beowulf*." *Studies in Popular Culture* 31, no. 2 (2009): 45–59.

Free Country: A Tale of the Children's Crusade, written by Neil Gaiman, Toby Litt, Rachel Pollack, Alisa Kwitney, and Jamie Delano, art by Chris Bachalo, Mike Barreiro, Peter Gross, Al Davison, and Peter Snejbjerg. Vertigo, 2015.

Friesen, Ilse E. *The Female Crucifix: Images of St. Wilgefortis since the Middle Ages*. Waterloo, Canada: Wilfrid Laurier University Press, 2001.

Fulk, R. D., Robert E. Bjork, and John D. Niles. Introduction to *Klaeber's "Beowulf" and the Fight at Finnsburg*. 4th ed. Toronto: University of Toronto Press, 2009, xxiii–cxc.

Gaiman, Neil. *American Gods*. 2001. 10th anniversary edition. New York: HarperCollins, 2011.

Gaiman, Neil. *The Annotated American Gods*. Edited by Leslie Klinger. New York: William Morrow, 2020.

Gaiman, Neil. *The Annotated Sandman*. 4 vols. Edited by Leslie Klinger. Burbank: DC Comics, 2012–15.

Gaiman, Neil. "Bay Wolf." 1998. In *Smoke and Mirrors*, 196–203.

Gaiman, Neil. *The Books of Magic*. John Bolton, Scott Hampton, Charles Vess, and Paul Johnson, artists. Burbank: DC Comics, 1993.

Gaiman, Neil. *Chivalry*. Illustrated by Colleen Doran. Milwaukie, OR: Dark Horse Comics, 2022.

Gaiman, Neil. "Chivalry." 1993. In *M Is for Magic*, 100–124. New York: HarperCollins, 2007.

Gaiman, Neil. *Fragile Things*. New York: HarperCollins, 2006.

Gaiman, Neil. "How Dare You: On America, and Writing about It." In *View from the Cheap Seats*, 64–66.

Gaiman, Neil. Introduction to *Fragile Things*, xvi–xxxiii.

Gaiman, Neil. Introduction to *The Quite Nice and Fairly Accurate "Good Omens" Script Book*, ix–xiii. London: Headline, 2019.

Gaiman, Neil. "Keepsakes and Treasures." 1999. In *Fragile Things*, 108–26.

Gaiman, Neil. "Make Good Art." In *View from the Cheap Seats*, 451–59.

Gaiman, Neil. "The Monarch of the Glen." In *Fragile Things*, 284–339.

Gaiman, Neil. "Neil Gaiman on Terry Pratchett." In *Good Omens: The Nice and Accurate Prophecies of Agnes Nutter, Witch*, 403–7. New York: HarperCollins, 2006.

Gaiman, Neil. *Neverwhere*. 1996. New York: Avon, 1997.

Gaiman, Neil. *Norse Mythology*. New York: Norton, 2017.

Gaiman, Neil. "October in the Chair." 2002. In *M Is for Magic*, 75–99. New York: HarperCollins, 2007.

Gaiman, Neil. *Odd and the Frost Giants*. Illustrated by Chris Riddell. New York: HarperCollins, 2016.

Gaiman, Neil. *Odd and the Frost Giants*. London: Bloomsbury, 2008.

Gaiman, Neil. "Of Meetings and Partings." In *This Mortal Mountain: The Collected Stories of Roger Zelazny*, edited by David Grubbs, Christopher Kovacs, and Anne Crimmins, 3:11–14. Boston: NESFA, 2009.

Gaiman, Neil. "Once Upon a Time." In *View from the Cheap Seats*, 423–29.

Gaiman, Neil. "Only the End of the World Again." In *Smoke and Mirrors*, 176–95.

Gaiman, Neil. "Ray Bradbury, *Fahrenheit 451* and What Science Fiction Is and Does." In *View from the Cheap Seats*, 177–82.

Gaiman, Neil. *The Sandman: Endless Nights*. 30th anniversary edition. Burbank: DC Comics, 2019.

Gaiman, Neil. *Sandman: The Wake*. 30th anniversary edition. Burbank: DC Comics, 2019.

Gaiman, Neil. *The Sleeper and the Spindle*. Illustrated by Chris Riddell. Harper, 2014.

Gaiman, Neil. *Smoke and Mirrors*. New York: Avon, 1998.

Gaiman, Neil. "Snow, Glass, Apples." In *Smoke and Mirrors*, 331–46.

Gaiman, Neil. "Some Reflections on Myth (With Several Digressions onto Gardening, Comics and Fairy Tales)." In *View from the Cheap Seats*, 54–63.

Gaiman, Neil. *Stardust*. Charles Vess, illustrator. Burbank: DC Comics, 1998.

Gaiman, Neil. *Stardust*. New York: HarperCollins, 1999.

Gaiman, Neil. *Trigger Warning*. New York: HarperCollins, 2015.

Gaiman, Neil. *The View from the Cheap Seats*. New York: William Morrow, 2016.

Gaiman, Neil, and Terry Pratchett. *Good Omens: The Nice and Accurate Prophecies of Agnes Nutter, Witch.* 1990. New York: HarperCollins, 2006.

Geoffrey of Monmouth. *The History of the Kings of Britain.* Edited and translated by Lewis Thorpe. London: Penguin, 1966.

Good Omens. TV series. Created by Neil Gaiman and Terry Pratchett. With David Tennant and Michael Sheen. Amazon Prime, 2019–23.

Gorman, Susan. "Neil Gaiman's *American Gods:* A Postmodern Epic for America." *Mythlore* 37, no. 1 (2018): 165–81. https://dc.swosu.edu/cgi/viewcontent.cgi?article=1191&context=mythlore.

Graham, Elaine. *Representations of the Post/human: Monsters, Aliens, and Others in Popular Culture.* New Brunswick, NJ: Rutgers University Press, 2002.

Guillaume de Lorris and Jean de Meun. *The Romance of the Rose.* Translated by Frances Horgan. Oxford: Oxford University Press, 1994.

Gutierrez, Anna Katrina. "Weaving New Dreams from Old Cloth: Conceptual Blending and Hybrid Identities in Neil Gaiman's Fairy-Tale Retellings." In Sommers and Eveleth, *Artistry of Neil Gaiman,* 217–33.

Hardiman, Phillipa. *Matter of Identity in Medieval Romance.* Woodbridge, UK: D. S. Brewer, 2002.

Haydock, Nickolas, and E. L. Risden, eds. *"Beowulf" on Film: Adaptations and Variations.* Jefferson, NC: McFarland, 2013.

Henshall, Kenneth. *Folly and Fortune in Early British History.* Palgrave, 2008.

Higham, Nicholas J. *King Arthur: The Making of a Legend.* New Haven, CT: Yale University Press, 2018.

Higham, Nicholas J., and Martin J. Ryan. *The Anglo-Saxon World.* New Haven, CT: Yale University Press, 2013.

Hodapp, William. "Arthur, Beowulf, Robin Hood, and Hollywood's Desire for Origins." *The Year's Work in Medievalism* 26 (2011): 66–89.

Hodapp, William. "'*No hie fæder cunnon*': But Twenty-First Century Film Makers Do." *Essays in Medieval Studies* 26 (2010): 101–8.

Hoogenboezem, Daphne M. "Medievalism and Magic: Illustrating Classical French Fairy Tales." In *Early Modern Medievalisms: The Interplay Between Scholarly Reflection and Artistic Production,* edited by Alicia Montoya, Sophie van Romburgh, and Wim van Anrooij, 249–83. Leiden: Brill, 2010.

Hughes, Kevin. *Constructing Antichrist: Paul, Biblical Commentary, and the Development of Doctrine in the Early Middle Ages.* Catholic University of America Press, 2005.

Hume, Kathryn. “Loki and Odin: Old Gods Repurposed by Neil Gaiman, A. S. Byatt, and Klas Östergren.” *Studies in the Novel* 51, no. 2 (2019): 297–310.

Hutton, Ronald. “The Making of the Early Modern British Fairy Tradition.” *Historical Journal* 57, no. 4 (2014): 1135–56.

Jahlmar, Joakim. “‘Give the Devil His Due’: Freedom, Damnation, and Milton’s *Paradise Lost* in Neil Gaiman’s *The Sandman: Season of Mists*.” *Partial Answers: Journal of Literature and the History of Ideas* 13, no. 2 (2015): 267–86.

Janega, Eleanor, and Neil Max Emmanuel. *The Middle Ages: A Graphic History*. Icon, 2021.

Joiner, Jorunn. “‘Valhalla Anew!’: Ragnarök, Cultural Networks, and National Identity in *American Gods*.” *Exclamat!on* 3 (2019): 124–43.

Jones, Chris. “From Heorot to Hollywood: *Beowulf* in its Third Millennium.” In *Anglo-Saxon Culture and the Medieval Imagination*, edited by David Clark and Nicholas Perkins, 13–29. Woodbridge, UK: Boydell & Brewer, 2017.

Kaufman, Amy S., and Paul B. Sturtevant. *The Devil’s Historians*. Toronto: University of Toronto Press, 2020.

Keightley, Thomas. *The Fairy Mythology*. George Bell, 1892. https://www.gutenberg.org/files/41006/41006-h/41006-h.htm.

Kershaw, Sylvia, and Laurie Ormond. “‘We Are the Monsters Now’: The Genre Medievalism of Robert Zemeckis’ *Beowulf*.” *Screening the Past* 26 (2009). http://tlweb.latrobe.edu.au/humanities/screeningthepast/26/early-europe/genre-medievalism-beowulf.html.

King, Pamela M. “Morality Plays.” In *The Cambridge Companion to Medieval English Theater*, edited by Richard Beadle, 240–64. Cambridge: Cambridge University Press, 1994.

King Arthur. Written by David Franzoni. Directed by Antoine Fuqua. Touchstone, 2004.

Klapcsik, Sándor. “Neil Gaiman’s Irony, Liminal Fantasies, and Fairy Tale Adaptations.” *Hungarian Journal of English and American Studies* 14, no. 2 (2008): 317–34.

Knight, Steven. “The Social Function of the Middle English Romances.” In *Medieval Literature: Criticism, Ideology, and History*, edited by David Aers, 99–122. New York: St. Martin’s Press, 1986.

Kolve, V. A. “*Everyman* and the Parable of the Talents.” In *The Medieval Drama*, edited by Sandro Sticca, 69–98. New York: State University of New York Press, 1972.

Kristeva, Julia. *The Powers of Horror: An Essay in Abjection.* Translated by Leon S. Roudeiz. New York: Columbia University Press, 1982.

Langland, William. *Piers Plowman. Old and Middle English c. 890–c.1450,* 3rd ed., edited by Elaine Treharne, 688–727. Hoboken, NJ: Wiley-Blackwell, 2002.

Larrington, Carolyne. Introduction to *The Poetic Edda,* edited and translated by Carolyne Larrington, x–xxv. Oxford: Oxford University Press, 1996.

Larrington, Carolyne. "Our Return to Twilight: The *Poetic Edda* and Our Renewed Relationship with Norse Myth." *Times Literary Supplement,* June 28, 2019.

Lavin, Talia. *Culture Warlords: My Journey into the Dark Web of White Supremacy.* Legacy Lit Books, 2020.

Law, Elizabeth. "The Fairest of All: Snow White and Gendered Power in 'Snow, Glass, Apples.'" In *Feminism in the Works of Neil Gaiman: Essays on the Comics, Poetry, and Prose,* edited by Tara Prescott and Aaron Drucker, 177–91. Jefferson, NC: McFarland, 2012.

Lindow, John. *Norse Mythology: A Guide to Gods, Heroes, Rituals, and Beliefs.* Oxford: Oxford University Press, 2002.

Lionarons, Joyce Tally. "*Beowulf:* Myth and Monsters." *English Studies* 77, no. 1 (1996): 1–14.

Lum, Jade. "Un-training the Imagination through Adaptation: An Exploration of Gender through Neil Gaiman's *The Sleeper and the Spindle.*" In *Contemporary Fairy-Tale Magic: Subverting Gender and Genre,* edited by Lydia Brugu and Auba Llompart, 44–53. Leiden: Brill, 2020.

Lybeaus Desconus. Edited by Eve Salisbury and James Weldon. Medieval Institute Publications, 2013. https://d.lib.rochester.edu/teams/publication/salisbury-and-weldon-lybeaus-desconus. Accessed February 8, 2023.

MacColl, Alan. "King Arthur and the Making of an English Britain." *History Today,* March 1999, 7–13.

Machan, Tim William. "Snorri's *Edda,* Mythology, and Anglo-Saxon Studies." *Modern Philology* 113, no. 3 (2016): 295–309.

Macrobius. *Commentary on the "Dream of Scipio."* Translated by William Harris Stahl. New York: Columbia University Press, 1952.

Maddox, Donald, and Sara Sturm-Maddox. Introduction to *Melusine,* by Jean d'Arras, 1–16. University Park: Pennsylvania State University Press, 2010.

Malory, Sir Thomas. *Le Morte Darthur.* Edited by Stephen H. A. Shepherd. New York: Norton, 2004.

Mankind. Edited by Kathleen M. Ashley and Gerard NeCastro. University of

Rochester, 2010. https://d.lib.rochester.edu/teams/publication/ashley-and-necastro-mankind. Accessed February 8, 2023.

Marie de France. *The Lays of Marie de France.* Translated by David R. Slavitt. Alberta, Canada: AU Press, 2013.

Matthews, David. *Medievalism: A Critical History.* Woodbridge, UK: Boydell & Brewer, 2015.

Melion, Walter S., and Bart Ramakers, eds. *Personification: Embodying Meaning and Emotion.* Leiden: Brill, 2016.

Mendelesohn, Farah, and Edward James. *A Short History of Fantasy.* 2nd ed. Oxfordshire, UK: Libri, 2012.

Milton, John. *Paradise Lost.* 1667. https://www.gutenberg.org/ebooks/26.

Mommsen, Thodore E. "Petrarch's Conception of the 'Dark Ages.'" *Speculum* 17, no. 2 (1942): 226–42.

Murray, James A. H. *The Romance and Prophecies of Thomas of Erceldonne.* Early English Text Society, 1875. https://books.google.com/books?id=GFEJAAAAQAAJ&pg=PP1.

Niles, John D. "Introduction: *Beowulf,* Truth, and Meaning." In A "*Beowulf*" *Handbook,* edited by Robert E. Bjork and John D. Niles, 1–12. Lincoln: University of Nebraska Press, 1997.

O'Hear, Natasha, and Anthony O'Hear. *Picturing the Apocalypse: The Book of Revelation in the Arts over Two Millennia.* Oxford: Oxford University Press, 2015.

Osmond, Andrew. Review of *Beowulf. Sight and Sound* 18, no. 1 (2008): 61.

The Poems of the "Pearl" Manuscript. 4th ed. Edited by Malcolm Andrew and Ronald Waldron. Exeter: University of Exeter Press, 2002.

The Poetic Edda. Edited and translated by Carolyne Larrington. Oxford: Oxford University Press, 1996.

Pollack, Rachel. *The Complete Illustrated Guide to Tarot.* Boston: Element, 1999.

Porter, Adam. "Neil Gaiman's Lucifer: Reconsidering Milton's Satan." *Journal of Religion and Popular Culture* 25, no. 2 (2013): 175–85.

Pugh, Tison. "Introduction: Disney's Retroprogressive Medievalisms: Where Yesterday Is Tomorrow Today." In Pugh and Aronstein, *Disney Middle Ages,* 1–20.

Pugh, Tison, and Angela Jane Weisl. *Medievalisms: Making the Past in the Present.* New York: Routledge, 2013.

Pugh, Tison, and Susan Aronstein, eds. *The Disney Middle Ages: A Fairy-Tale and Fantasy Past.* London: Palgrave Macmillan, 2012.

Purkiss, Diane. *At the Bottom of the Garden: A Dark History of Fairies, Hobgoblins, and Other Troublesome Things*. New York: New York University Press, 2000.

Rauch, Stephen. *Neil Gaiman's "The Sandman" and Joseph Campbell: In Search of the Modern Myth*. Cabin John, MD: Wildside, 2003.

Rider, Jeff. "The Other Worlds of Romance." In *The Cambridge Companion to Medieval Literature*, edited by Roberta Krueger, 115–31. Cambridge: Cambridge University Press, 2000.

Risden, E. L. "The Cinematic Commoditization of *Beowulf*: The Serial Fetishizing of a Hero." In Haydock and Risden, *"Beowulf" on Film*, 66–80.

Risden, E. L. "Heroic Humor in *Beowulf*." In *Humour in Anglo-Saxon Literature*, edited by Jonathan Wilcox, 71–78. Woodbridge, UK: D. S. Brewer, 2000.

Robinson, Fred C. "Beowulf." In *The Cambridge Companion to Old English Literature*, edited by Malcom Godden and Michael Lapidge, 142–59. Cambridge: Cambridge University Press, 1986.

Robinson, Fred C. *Beowulf and the Appositive Style*. Knoxville: University of Tennessee Press, 1985.

Roman, Christopher. "The Use of Nature: Representing Religion in Medieval Film." In *Neomedievalism in the Media*, edited by Carol L. Robinson and Pamela Clements, 55–81. Lewiston, NY: Edwin Mellen, 2012.

Russell, Danielle. "Damsels in Deep Rest No More: The Coalescence of Light and Dark in *Blueberry Girl*, *The Wolves in the Walls*, and *The Sleeper and the Spindle*." In Sommers and Eveleth, *Artistry of Neil Gaiman*, 169–84.

Russell, Stephen J. *The English Dream Vision: Anatomy of a Form*. Columbus: Ohio State University Press, 1988.

Salisbury, Eve, and James Weldon. Introduction to *Lybeaus Desconus*. Medieval Institute Publications, 2013. https://d.lib.rochester.edu/teams/text/salisbury-and-weldon-lybeaus-desconus-introduction. Accessed February 8, 2023.

The Sandman. TV series. Created by Neil Gaiman. With Tom Sturridge. Netflix, 2022–.

Schweitzer, Darrell. "Tapdancing on the Shoulders of Giants: Gaiman's *Stardust* and Its Antecedents." In *The Neil Gaiman Reader*, edited by Darrell Schweitzer, 115–21. Cabin John, MD: Wildside, 2007.

Scott, Daniel. "*And the World Continues to Spin. . . .*: Secularism and Demystification in *Good Omens*." In *Terry Pratchett's Narrative Worlds: From Giant Turtles to Small Gods*, edited by Marion Rana, 73–91. London: Palgrave Macmillan, 2018.

Selling, Kim. "'Fantastic Neomedievalism': The Image of the Middle Ages in Popular Fantasy." In *Flashes of the Fantastic: Selected Essays from the "War of the Worlds" Centennial: Nineteenth International Conference on the Fantastic in the Arts*, edited by David Ketterer, 211–18. Westport, CT: Praeger, 2004.

Sheinfeld, Shayna. "Scenes from the End of the World in American Popular Culture." In *The Oxford Handbook of the Bible and American Popular Culture*, edited by Dan W. Clanton and Terry R. Clark, 201–18. Oxford: Oxford University Press, 2020.

Simpson, J. R. "King Arthur's Enchanted Sleep: Early Nineteenth Century Legends." *Folklore* 97, no. 2 (1986): 206–9.

Sleeping Beauty. Written by Erdman Penner. Directed by Clyde Geroimi. Walt Disney Productions, 1959.

Snorri Sturluson. *The Prose Edda*. Edited and translated by Jesse Byock. London: Penguin, 2005.

Sodeman, Jesper Skytte. "*American Gods* and Where to Find Them: Modern Myth and Material Experience." *Journal of Comparative Literature and Aesthetics* 42 (2019): 59–73.

Sommers, Joseph Michael, ed. *Conversations with Neil Gaiman*. Jackson: University Press of Mississippi, 2018.

Sommers, Joseph Michael, and Kyle Eveleth, eds. *The Artistry of Neil Gaiman: Finding Light in the Shadows*. Jackson: University Press of Mississippi, 2019.

Spearing, A. C. *Medieval Dream-Poetry*. Cambridge: Cambridge University Press, 1976.

Stardust. Written by Matthew Vaughn and Jane Goldman. Directed by Matthew Vaughn. Paramount, 2007.

Steele, Robert, and Dorothea Waley Singer. "The Emerald Table." *Proceedings of the Royal Society of Medicine* 21, no. 3 (1928): 41–57.

Sturtevant, Paul. "'You Don't Learn It Deliberately, but You Just Know It from What You've Seen': British Understandings of the Medieval Past Gleaned from Disney's Fairy Tales." In Pugh and Aronstein, *Disney Middle Ages*, 77–96.

The Summoning of Everyman. University of Michigan, 1993. https://quod.lib.umich.edu/c/cme/Everyman/. Accessed February 8, 2023.

The 13th Warrior. Written by William Wisher Jr. and Warren Lewis. Directed by John McTiernan. Touchstone, 1999.

Thorpe, Lewis, ed. Introduction to *History of the Kings of Britain*, by Geoffrey of Monmouth, 1–45. London: Penguin, 1966.

Tolkien, J. R. R. "*Beowulf*: The Monsters and the Critics." In *"The Monsters and the Critics" and Other Essays*, edited by Christopher Tolkien, 5–48. New York: HarperCollins, 2006.

Tolkien, J. R. R. "On Fairy-Stories." In *"The Monsters and the Critics" and Other Essays*, edited by Christopher Tolkien, 109–61. New York: HarperCollins, 2006.

Tolmie, Jane. "Medievalism and the Fantasy Heroine." *Journal of Gender Studies* 15, no. 2 (2006): 145–58.

Ussher, Jane M. *Managing the Monstrous Feminine: Regulating the Reproductive Body*. New York: Routledge, 2006.

Wade, James. *Fairies in Medieval Romance*. London: Palgrave Macmillan, 2011.

Walkden, George. "The Status of *hwæt* in Old English." *English Language and Linguistics* 17, no. 3 (2013): 465–88.

Wanner, Kevin J. "Cunning Intelligence in Norse Myth: Loki, Óðinn, and the Limits of Sovereignty." *History of Religions* 48, no. 3 (2009): 211–46.

Warner, Marina. *From the Beast to the Blonde: On Fairy Tales and Their Tellers*. New York: Noonday, 1994.

Watkins, John. "The Allegorical Theatre: Moralities, Interludes, and Protestant Drama." In *The Cambridge History of Medieval Literature*, edited by David Wallace, 767–92. Cambridge: Cambridge University Press, 2002.

Whyman, Matt. *The Nice and Accurate "Good Omens" TV Companion*. New York: William Morrow, 2019.

Winslade, Jason Lawton. "Enrolling in the 'Hidden School': Timothy Hunter and the Education of the Teenage Comic Book Magus." In *Supernatural Youth: The Rise of the Teen Hero in Literature and Popular Culture*, edited by Jes Battis, 197–215. Lanham, MD: Lexington, 2011.

Wolfe, Gary K. "Neil Gaiman." In *Supernatural Fiction Writers: Contemporary Fantasy and Horror*, edited by Richard Bleiler, 369–75. New York: Charles Scribner's Sons, 2003.

Wulfstan. "Sermo Lupi ad Anglos." In *Old and Middle English, c. 890–c. 1450: An Anthology*, 3rd ed., edited by Elaine Treharne, 260–67. Hoboken, NJ: Wiley-Blackwell, 2010.

Younus, Zainab. "(Re)interpreting Dante's *Inferno* in Gaiman's *Season of*

Mists." In *Framescapes: Graphic Narrative Intertexts*, edited by Mikhail Peppas and Sanabelle Ebrahim, 85–92. Whitney, UK: Inter-disciplinary, 2016.

Zelazny, Roger. Introduction to *The Books of Magic*, by Neil Gaiman. Burbank: DC Comics, 1993, ii–iv.

Ziolkowski, Jan M. *Fairy Tales from Before Fairy Tales: The Medieval Latin Past of Wonderful Lies*. Ann Arbor: University of Michigan Press, 2009.

Zipes, Jack. *Victorian Fairy Tales: The Revolt of the Fairies and Elves*. New York: Routledge, 1987.

INDEX